What People Are Saying About
OWN THE FUTURE

"As I reread the pages, the words go deeper. The message becomes more powerful. This isn't just a book, it's a transmission.

It gave me a path forward when I was lost. A real mentor, with real answers to real problems.

What Renner shares in this book is transformative. It's rare to find someone who not only knows the system, but who can explain it clearly enough to help others rise through it.

I will always be grateful, for this transformation, for this clarity, and for the freedom I'm now beginning to feel."

- **Shlomie Hoffman,** CEO - Hoffman Financial Team

"Life is a journey of becoming; becoming who you were meant to be, becoming the mountain.

It is a blend of building yourself up and elevating your spirit to heights once thought impossible, until you stepped into the right rooms, until your vision united others to build something greater than themselves, until your dreams grew so big that the only path left was forward, upward, and onward.

This book is not a formula.

It is the essence of growth, life, and true success."

- **Kenneth Brenneman,** Founder - Crest Performance Partners LLC

"This isn't just a book. It's a blueprint forged in fire. Every page carries the weight of lived experience... Not imagined theory -from a man who built when others quit. If you've ever felt underestimated or overlooked, this is your playbook for reclaiming power."

- **Saber J. Christensen,** Author of "The Branches of Yggdrasil"

*"This is not a book about winning.
It is a book about awakening.
It's the moment you stop playing by rules you never agreed to,
and begin designing the life, the work, and the legacy that only you can build.*

*The real revolution isn't in chasing success.
It's in questioning the script, rewriting the rules,
and becoming the architect of a system that no longer asks for your permission.*

*Growth does not come from compliance. It comes from clarity.
From the courage to leave the mountain you were told to climb,
and the conviction to build one worthy of those who will follow in your steps."*

- **Oscar Felipe,** Co-Founder & CEO - FORT Group LLC, Board Member of ArtIn Energy.

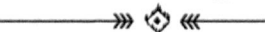

"Only someone who has truly lived through the setbacks, betrayals, and quiet rebuilds could write a book like this.

OWN THE FUTURE doesn't just offer strategies.
It breaks the illusion of the game itself.

It comes from someone who's stepped outside the system and sees it for what it really is.

This book won't land with everyone, but for those who carry talent, vision, and the weight of never quite fitting in, it's a mirror, a compass, and a quiet call to rise. It's honest, unfiltered, and deeply human.
You can't fake this kind of clarity.
And I don't believe it can be copied. I do believe it will change lives."

- **Simon Han**, Co-founder & Principal - Elevate Integrated Solution Ltd. Senior Partner - ArtIn Energy.

OWN *THE* FUTURE

A Journey Through the Hidden World of Wealth, Power, and Freedom

OWN THE FUTURE

A Journey Through the Hidden World
of Wealth, Power, and Freedom

*"This book is not about motivation.
It's about mechanics, the real systems behind
power, wealth, and legacy.
No fluff.
No gatekeeping.
Just everything they never wanted you to know."*

KL RENNER
Founder of FORT Group LLC,
TRIVIX Group LLC, Othralis LLC,
And Mythara Studios LLC

PUBLISHED BY TORCHLINE PRESS

TORCHLINE PRESS

Copyright © 2025 by Torchline Media LLC.
All rights reserved.

Project editor: Suzanne Christensen
Cover design and Interior design: Othralis LLC
Illustrations: Property of Othralis LLC

No part of this book may be copied, stored in a retrieval system, or transmitted in any form or by any means: electronic, mechanical, photocopying, recording, or otherwise, without the prior written permission of the publisher, except for brief quotations used in critical articles or reviews.

This book is for informational and educational purposes only. The author and publisher are not engaged in rendering legal, tax, investment, or financial advice. The ideas and strategies contained herein may not be suitable for every individual or situation. The reader should consult with a licensed professional where appropriate.

Every effort has been made to ensure the accuracy of the content. However, laws and business practices evolve, and the author makes no representations or warranties about the accuracy, applicability, or completeness of the content in this book. The author and publisher disclaim any liability, loss, or risk incurred as a consequence, directly or indirectly, from the use and application of any of the contents of this work.

Names and identifying details may have been changed to protect privacy.
Library of Congress Control Number: 2025919470
Hardcover Jacketed ISBN: 979-8-9995582-0-6
Hardcover Case Laminate ISBN: 979-8-9995582-2-0
Hardcover Collector's Edition ISBN: 979-8-9995582-9-9
Paperback ISBN: 979-8-9995582-1-3
E-book ISBN: 979-8-9995582-4-4
Audiobook ISBN: 979-8-9995582-3-7
1st Edition August 2025
Printed in the United States of America.

Published in the United States by: Torchline Press
an imprint of Torchline Media LLC
www.TorchlinePress.com
KL Renner is a pen name of Jeremy L. Christensen.
Torchline Press and the Torchline mark are trademarks of Torchline Media LLC.

AI & Machine Learning Notice:
This book, its structure, contents, and language are protected under copyright law. No portion of this work, in any form, may be used in the training, fine-tuning, ingestion, or processing by artificial intelligence or machine learning systems, including large language models (LLMs), without the express written consent of the copyright holder.

*For the ones who saw through the system early.
For the ones who never stopped asking why.
And for the ones who were told to wait... but didn't.*

Contents

Foreword -- 6

Author's Note - Collector's Edition ------------------------ 8

Disclaimer -- 10

Chapter 1: The Right Room --------------------------------- 13

Chapter 2: The Rules They Never Taught You ------------- 25

Chapter 3: The Language Of Leverage --------------------- 33

Chapter 4: Designing The Mountain ------------------------ 41

Chapter 5: Building in the Dark ---------------------------- 47

Chapter 6: Tests And Allies -------------------------------- 55

Chapter 7: The Ordeal -------------------------------------- 63

Chapter 8: The Reward ------------------------------------- 73

Chapter 9: The Road Back ---------------------------------- 81

Chapter 10: The Shift Back --------------------------------- 89

Chapter 11: The Shift From Momentum To Meaning ----- 97

Chapter 12: The Hardest Part No One Talks About ----- 105

Chapter 13: The Shift From Growth To Uplift ----------- 113

Chapter 14: How To Leave Without Losing Yourself --- 119

Chapter 15: Legacy In Real Time -------------------------- 125

Before We Begin

CHAPTER 16: THE WEIGHT OF THE TORCH ---------------------133

EPILOGUE: THE BEGINNING------------------------------------141

APPENDIX I --144

APPENDIX II ---148

APPENDIX III --153

VISUAL FRAMEWORK:--155

OWN THE FUTURE

BEFORE WE BEGIN

"This isn't a business book. It's a reckoning."

This book isn't for the ones playing it safe.
It's not for the perfectly packaged.
Not for those who've made peace with "good enough."
It's for the restless. The ones who toss and turn, seeing through the cracks in the system.
The builders who work with shaking hands and swollen eyes.
The ones who carry their vision like a scar, too personal to ignore, too raw to explain.
You know who you are. You've worn the mask.
Sat through meetings that drained something you couldn't name.
Built businesses while second-guessing your own worth.
Looked successful on paper,
while quietly unraveling behind the scenes.
You've climbed ladders only to realize they leaned against the wrong wall.
You've sacrificed time, family, health - not for ego, but because you believed.
And now, maybe, you're wondering if belief is enough.
This book is my offering to that moment.
It was born at the crossroads, where vision collides with exhaustion, where legacy tangles with identity, and where power stops looking like power.
I didn't write it as a manual. I wrote it as a mirror.
Because no one tells you that building something meaningful will break you before it builds you.
That leadership will expose you more than it exalts you.
That freedom is a heavier weight than obedience ever was.

OWN THE FUTURE

But you'll also learn this:
There is no map. Only questions. Only scars.
Only the people who walk with you or rise because you did.
So, if you're tired of advice and hungry for truth:
welcome.
If you've been pretending to be further ahead than you are:
welcome.
If you're done being the tool and ready to become the
architect: welcome.
You're not alone. You're just early.
You're not broken. You're becoming.
This isn't just a business book.
It's a survival guide for those called to build in a world that
doesn't always see them coming.
It's not linear. It's layered.
You'll find frameworks, yes. Tools. Questions. Language
you can steal.
But more importantly, you'll find permission.
Permission to let go.
Permission to step up.
Permission to evolve.
You don't have to read this like a textbook.
You can dog-ear it, argue with it, cry on it.
You can skip chapters and come back later.
You can start from the middle.
Because this isn't sacred. You are.
So take what you need.
Leave what you don't.
But whatever you do:
Don't let the next version of you die because the current
version is too scared to let go.
If anything here resonates,
that means you're not at the end.
You're just getting started.

Foreword

By Saber, Co-Founder and Son

If you're holding this book, you've likely already felt it: the system is rigged.

Not against the talented or the willing, but against the underestimated.

Against the ones who didn't come from pedigree, didn't speak in pitch decks, and didn't wait for permission.

This isn't a book about chasing dreams.

It's a manual for reclaiming power, one brutal, brilliant, battle-tested principle at a time.

I've worked alongside Jeremy for years. He's my business partner, but more importantly, he's my father.

I lived half this book with him. That's what made writing this foreword so difficult. Because I didn't just read it... I *remembered* it.

I've seen him lose everything. I've seen him go through hell, only to architect the next chapter while most people would still be licking their wounds.

I've seen him carry vision when the room went quiet, when partners bailed, when banks turned cold, and when the math didn't make sense to anyone but him.

That kind of leadership doesn't come from theory.

It comes from fire.

And fire leaves a mark.

This book?

It's that mark.

Every page is a code: earned, not imagined.

He doesn't write to impress. He writes to transfer. To hand you a key.

Not the kind of key they hand out in Ivy League lecture halls or on startup stages in Silicon Valley.

But the kind you forge when you've bled on the blueprint and still decided to keep building.

There's no fluff here. No recycled inspiration. Just hard-won truths, written by someone who's chosen the long, ugly, righteous road of actual ownership.

And let me tell you, when you build like that, you don't just create wealth.

You create permanence.

You'll see the name KL Renner on the cover, but to me, it'll always be Dad.

And this book? It's everything I watched him become.

If you've ever felt like the rules weren't made for people like you, this book will show you how to write new ones.

If you've been burned by loyalty, confused by opportunity, or overwhelmed by the sheer pressure of holding a vision others can't see, this is your field guide.

Read this like your future depends on it.

Because it might.

And when you're finished, don't just nod.

Build.

- Saber

Author's Note

I didn't write this to impress anyone.

I wrote it because I wish someone had written it for me.

Not a how-to manual. Not a highlight reel.

A real map: marked by detours, scars, and the kind of questions that shake you awake.

Most of what you're about to read isn't taught in school.

It's not in your MBA curriculum, and it's not handed out in corporate onboarding packets.

The truth? It's barely whispered, even in the "right" rooms, unless you already were approved to be in those rooms.

These are the mechanics of wealth, power, and legacy; stripped of fluff, hype, and gatekeeping.

They've been carved from real pressure:

Government contracts.

Billion-dollar projects.

Backroom betrayals.

Sleepless rebuilds.

Film negotiations.

And more than a few nights sleeping in a car, wondering how the hell I'd climb back out.

This book is part story, part playbook, and part rebellion.

It's for anyone tired of playing small. Anyone who's done everything "right" and still feels stuck. Anyone who can feel the weight of potential but has never been given the tools to unlock it.

You don't need another motivational quote.

You need better questions.

A sharper lens.

A reason to stop waiting and start building.

The world doesn't need more followers.

It needs more architects.

Author's Note

More builders.
Some of these lessons cost me millions.
Others sent me back to zero.
You?
You get them in a single book.
Hopefully you haven't lost millions or been betrayed to the point of losing everything.
So don't just read this.
Use it.
Mark it up.
Challenge it.
Make it your own.
Take what serves you and leave the rest behind.
This isn't the story of how I won. It's the strategy of how I refused to quit.
This edition is for you.
Let's begin.

- / KL RENNER

DISCLAIMER

A NOTE ON NAMES AND STORIES

The experiences, scenarios, and lessons in this book are all real. The names, however, are not.
In some cases, they've been changed to protect privacy.
In others, they've been withheld out of respect, even for those who caused harm.
This isn't a book about revenge. It's about rebuilding. And no one rises by dragging others down.
If you recognize yourself in these pages, I hope it's in the lessons, not the labels.
This story was never about the drama.
It's about what you do after.

The
Open Door

Access begins with awareness.

Chapter 1
The Right Room

*"There is no magic in the system.
It's just being asked the right questions.
If you've never been exposed to the right people,
you've never been asked the right questions."*

I didn't learn the system was rigged from a book. It wasn't a TED Talk revelation or podcast epiphany.

I lived it... felt it... in a stale government office tucked inside a nondescript high-rise in downtown Salt Lake City. The hum of fluorescent lights matched the dull drone of the HVAC rattling the blinds behind Bill, a mid-level administrator with a handshake that felt firm but rehearsed, his smile as empty as the office decor.

It was late afternoon, that awkward stretch of day when coffee wears off and the room feels colder, emptier somehow. Bill listened as I walked him through a carefully prepared legislative package. Solid ROI, undeniable community impact, everything lined up perfectly.

But when I finished, he didn't ask questions. Didn't nod approval. Instead, he leaned back, glancing past me toward the hallway, and softly said, 'Renner, your plan is strong, really strong. But... we're moving forward with Barry's group. You understand, right?'

That was it. No critique. No counteroffer. Just a decision already made. A deal already promised.

And I realized... I wasn't pitching a plan. I was playing a part in a scene that had already been cast.

Deals didn't move because they worked.
They moved because someone whispered the right words to the right person, behind the right door, at just the right time.

Pause here.

When did you first realize the room was already decided before you entered it?

We all have a moment like that, not when we lost the deal, but when we realized we were never actually in the running.

That moment doesn't break you.

It wakes you up.

A clean pitch didn't matter.

A strong proposal? Irrelevant.

Merit didn't move money. Familiarity did. Loyalty. Leverage.
Proximity.

I watched a lesser proposal from Barry's team get greenlit, not because it had better numbers, but because they played golf once a month and sealed a handshake deal that served them both.

That's when it clicked: outcomes were being decided long before the meetings ever started.

Once I saw that, everything changed.

Not in anger, but in focus.

Something in me snapped, but not the way most people expect.

I didn't storm out. I didn't argue. I just sat there, still smiling, nodding at Bill like I understood. But inside, I was burning. Not because I'd lost the deal. But because I'd been naïve enough to think the deal was still on the table.

That was the moment I stopped trying to win the game they handed me.

And started learning how to build my own board.

Because once you see how the game actually works, you stop showing up like a stranger.

You stop hoping that effort alone is enough.

You stop mistaking silence for fairness.

You start moving like a designer.

And it begins with one shift: better questions.

Always.

Back then, I didn't have those questions.

I didn't even know what I didn't know.

I wasn't in the room where real decisions were made. I was in the corner, building programs and decks for people who already had the answers, already knew the outcome, already shook hands weeks before I showed up.

But I couldn't see it then.

Not fully.

I just remembered that strange feeling in the room.

The way someone would glance across the table with a look I wasn't meant to catch.

The unspoken rhythm that I couldn't read.

That moment when everyone else nodded in silent agreement…

and I sat there, smiling, clueless... thinking I still had a shot.

Before billion-dollar deals, before ownership and leverage, I was in the grind. Repossession. Bounty hunting. Fast money. Good money. Three to five hundred a car. Ten cars some days. Paid in cash. Paid fast. But that wasn't where it started. In the late nineties, I was trying to get a job. I had the skills. I had the qualifications. I got the interviews. But I didn't get the offers.

Too many times, I was told plainly that the company had chosen someone else because they would "give them a point."

I remember one interview in particular. I had crushed every question. The hiring manager, Jim, told me I was one of the strongest candidates they'd seen. But a week later, I got the call. "We're moving in another direction," he said. "You were great, but there's an internal initiative that favors certain hires." He didn't say it directly, but I heard it anyway: they needed the optics. Not the alignment. Just the checkbox. And I watched opportunities pass by. Bills began to pile up. My credit took a hit. Late payments, missed payment notices, snowballing interest. And suddenly, because my credit was bad, I became "unhireable." Now I wasn't just being passed over. I was being shut out.

That was the beginning of a different kind of path. One I didn't choose. One that chose me. I had to go out on my own. It felt like exile. It felt like a curse. But it was a gift. It forced me to ask better questions. It forced me to find the right people. And eventually, it put me in rooms where others asked better questions of me.

That's when everything changed.

But back then? I was still in survival mode.

I was doing repos, practically living in a tow truck. Sleeping maybe four hours a night, if that. I had a stack of printouts from banks and lenders: addresses, VINs, last-seen locations. I'd drive from street to street, alley to alley, scanning driveways and side lots, looking for the right vehicle. Sometimes I got lucky. Sometimes I just circled for hours, chasing ghosts.

There was no paycheck, only pickups. Three hundred here. Five hundred there. Cash, quick.

Enough to keep the tank full and the wheels moving.

But it wasn't living. It was survival. Barely.

Then a major client vanished.

Not because the work stopped. Not because we failed.

But because someone didn't like how much we were earning.

My business partner and I walked in like we always did, turning in the previous day's paperwork and expecting payment, just like every other day. We handed the invoices across the counter.

The interim GM, *Stacy*, looked at them... and hesitated.

"Yeah... I don't think we're going to pay this."

Just like that.

No reason. No warning. Just a wall.

My partner didn't let it slide. She spoke up, firm, direct, holding the line. We had done the work. We had earned it. And we weren't walking away empty-handed.

Stacy sighed, looked down at the invoices again, and said:

"Fine. But this is the final payment. We're done after this."

And just like that, we were cut off.

Work delivered. Contract canceled. No warning. No conversation. Just a quiet execution.

No cushion. No fallback. Nothing to land on.

The Right Room

I thought I was building a business. But I was building a treadmill; one I've watched a hundred other first-time founders build too. All momentum. No leverage. I once advised a client who had nearly half a million in yearly revenue and had no peace. One missed payment from a client nearly wrecked him. Not because he did anything wrong, but because the foundation was fragile.

I didn't just see it in him, I saw it in me.

And I knew I couldn't stay blind to it anymore.

It hit like a truck that the treadmill only worked if everyone else played fair.

And that day, they didn't.

I wasn't just out of money. I was out of momentum.

No safety net. No fallback. No backup plan.

I had built the entire operation on that contract. Thought I was building a business. But I wasn't.

I was building a treadmill, one that only worked if I ran nonstop.

And when one piece broke, it didn't just stop.

It launched me face-first into reality.

No savings. No equity. No leverage.

Just speed, and the illusion that speed meant progress.

I was moving fast, but I wasn't moving forward.

I was exhausted, but I wasn't getting anywhere.

Burning fuel and time, burning out, just to stay in the same place.

It wasn't growth.

It was survival in disguise.

The grooming starts early.

Before you can spell ambition.

You get worksheets and bubble tests. Told they will help "discover your future." But they are not looking for potential. They are looking for compliance. Your results? Maintenance worker. Dental assistant. Warehouse supervisor. Never founder. Never investor. Never architect of anything. You are told to be realistic. To dream within reach. To stay inside the lines drawn by someone else.

The schools never mention capital growth. Never define ownership. Never spoke a word about leverage.

In affluent communities, other circles, other networks? Those kids are learning from a different playbook. They are asked the kind of questions that shift futures. They are not told to wait. They are challenged to move.

And that's the secret: The right questions change your entire life.

But most people never hear them. Not because they aren't smart. But because they are never in the right room. They are never asked the right questions. That's the power of proximity. The acceleration of exposure. And once you hear those questions; real questions, challenging questions, expansive questions, you can't go back.

If you followed the plan, worked hard, stayed consistent, and it still feels like you're losing? You're not the problem. You're not lazy. You're not broken. You're operating inside a machine that is not designed for your freedom. It is built for your obedience.

We start by stopping the bleed.

If you're in debt, fix that first.

I remember hiding from phone calls. Dodging unknown numbers. Running the mental math every time I looked at a gas pump.

That's not laziness. That's survival mode.

And no one builds a future while bleeding out.

Not with shame. Not with fear.

With strategy.

If you are not in debt, I ask something few people ever hear: What do you need to feel clear again? Not what they expect from you. What do you need to feel free?

We strip away the noise. Not to punish. To regain control.

The Right Room

Because when you own your life again, you stop reacting. You start designing. But here is what no one says: You must improve your environment. You need new rooms. Rooms where questions elevate you. Where ownership is normal. Where clarity is the floor, not the ceiling.

I'll never forget one of the first right rooms I stepped into.

It was a private gathering in Park City. I didn't belong there, at least, that's how it felt. Everyone was polished. Quiet confidence. Generational wealth. But when I spoke, David, an angel investor twice my age, leaned in and said: "You saw something the rest of us missed."

That single sentence shifted me. Not because it gave me permission.

But because it showed me proximity wasn't out of reach.

When you sit at those tables, the questions change.

And eventually, so do you.

That period of rejection still shapes how I see the world today.

It sharpened my sense of justice and clarified the difference between being qualified and being chosen. I saw firsthand how surface-level narratives and bureaucratic scoring systems were more powerful than skill, effort, or integrity. It taught me that if you want freedom, you cannot wait for someone else to hand it to you. You have to build it with your own hands. That experience didn't just inform my work. It created my work.

It became the fire behind every strategy I design, every system I question, and every person I help empower. I do not carry bitterness from those years. I carry vision. I carry a blueprint that was carved from real struggle, and I use it to help others stop waiting for the world to see their worth, and start building proof that no one can ignore.

When I started stepping into better rooms, I noticed something strange. The best players weren't rushing. They weren't chasing. They weren't burning out. They were still in motion. But the pace was different. The power was different. They were not competing for access. They were writing the invitations.

They asked better questions. They structured deals that paid twice. They did not ask how to open the gate. They asked how to own the gate. And that changed everything. I stopped climbing ladders I did not choose. I stopped running games I didn't create. I began to build. From the ground up. With rules that honored my values. With leverage that belonged to me.

This is where your story begins. Not with a how-to guide. Not with someone handing you a key. It begins with clarity. Clarity that the system is real, but not sacred. Clarity that design is not reserved for the elite. Clarity that your freedom starts when you stop renting your time.

You don't need another guru. You need a decision.

This book won't save you. It will confront you.

To see differently. To think deeper. To act with intention.

It will give you the tools.

But the power? That stays with you.

Because one decision - ONE - can shift everything.

And once you move, your story doesn't wait.

It rewrites itself in real time.

From here on out, we're not surviving the system.

We're building one that belongs to us.

Not because we were chosen.

But because we finally chose ourselves.

And if you've ever wondered whether you belong in the room...

this is your proof.

The Right Room

I'm living proof you don't need to be born into the system to become the builder of it.

.:. - I used to think I was just unlucky. That if I worked hard enough, prepared well enough, I'd eventually break through. But I wasn't losing because I lacked skill. I was losing because I was in the wrong rooms, playing by the wrong rules.

Everything changed the instant that clicked. Not right away. Not flawlessly. Enough to recognize the system for what it was, however.

There is more to this chapter than rejection. It has to do with revelation.

Even though it was painful, that clarity turned into my first true asset.

Because you don't ask for permission once you understand how the game is played.

You begin creating your own table design.

You never again view a closed door in the same manner.

Because being in the right room does more than simply alter your chances.

It changes your questions.

And your questions shape everything that follows.

The
Hidden Script

Power favors those who can read between the lines.

Chapter 2
The Rules They Never Taught You

*"Most rules are never written,
they're just enforced."*

Clarity gets you in the door. But once you're inside, you realize something else: the room has rules no one has written down, and no one plans to explain to you.

I used to think I just needed to try harder. When deals fell through, when partnerships turned silent, when someone less qualified got the opportunity, I assumed I missed something. A detail. A cue. Maybe I just wasn't in the right place at the right time. But time kept passing. And the pattern kept repeating.

Then I found myself in a state conference room, across from a man and woman, who smiled like they already knew the outcome. We were negotiating a multi-million-dollar film incentive finance deal. I had the numbers. I had the structure. I had the edge. And I still lost. Not because I was wrong. But because I didn't understand the rules of the room.

I remember pitching what I thought was a bulletproof plan. The numbers worked. The outcome was real. I had endorsements, community support, everything lined up.

They listened, nodded, smiled. Then a month later, I saw my same plan moving forward, but with a different name on it.

They didn't outwork me. They outpositioned me.

That's when it clicked: I wasn't playing a merit-based game.

I was walking into rooms where the rules were already written, and wasn't even holding the playbook.

They weren't better. They were just fluent in a different game. A game with fewer handshakes and more signals. Where everything from the timing of a pause to the arrangement of seats meant something. Where the terms were written in posture, not paperwork.

They knew how to take up space, not with volume, but with presence. They knew which numbers mattered and which ones were just theater. And didn't just negotiate terms; they negotiated the frame.

I walked out stunned. I hadn't just lost a deal. I'd been speaking the wrong language.

It took years to see it clearly. To realize there was a hidden layer. A second playbook. A language of power, timing, and presence that most people never get taught, unless someone shows them. And even then, only if they're ready to see it.

Pause here.
What rules are you following that no one actually said out loud?
What have you assumed was fair,
just because it's common?

The day you realize there's a whole second conversation happening in every room, that's the day you stop playing checkers and start learning chess.

We're told early on that the world works a certain way. Work hard, and you'll be rewarded. Wait your turn. Keep your head down. Be dependable. Don't challenge authority. It sounds noble. Like a recipe for respect. But it's not how power actually works.

Because the real world doesn't reward obedience. It rewards ownership. It doesn't reward the quiet. It rewards those who control the room. It doesn't reward hard work alone. It rewards the ability to set the terms.

I've watched brilliant people get passed over because they followed the plan. And I've watched average people win big, not because they were smarter, but because they knew how to get in the right room, frame the conversation, and own the game.

The rules we're taught are rarely the ones that matter. They're safe. Predictable. Designed for stability. But power doesn't live in stability. It lives in motion. In disruption. In knowing how to pivot, reframe, and redirect the current.

The people who thrive in this world aren't just doing more: they're playing a different game entirely. One where the scoreboard isn't public. One where the win happens before the meeting even starts.

I remember a moment when someone finally asked me a question that shifted everything: "Are you chasing the deal, do you even know what the rules of the room are?" That one question made me pause. It reframed everything. I realized I was still reacting to offers instead of architecting outcomes.

That's what this chapter is about: the invisible script. The real game underneath the rules. And how to finally stop waiting to be picked... and start learning how to choose yourself.

I was invited to sit in on a deal as an observer. I wasn't leading. I wasn't even needed. But I watched everything. Two men, both worth more than a hundred million. One from oil. One from film. They were finalizing a joint venture. No pitch deck. No resume. No fifteen-slide presentations. Just questions. Just posture. Just leverage.

And one line from that meeting still echoes in my mind. One of them leaned back, sipped his coffee, and said:

"I don't mind giving up a few points as long as I control the vote."

That was it. No resistance. No pushback. They both understood the real game: control, not credit.

It hit me like a truck.

I had spent years fighting to prove myself, chasing percentages, climbing ladders. And in fifteen words, I saw it all for what it was.

The people who win don't chase the spotlight. They control the terms.

A few months later, I found myself in a negotiation where I finally flipped the frame. The other side was focused on valuation and equity. But I redirected the conversation toward decision rights and structuring voting power around creative direction. I didn't walk out with the biggest slice. But I walked out with the steering wheel.

Every successful person I know broke at least one of the rules we were taught in school. Not recklessly. Intentionally. They knew what they were trading. They didn't ask, "What job should I get?" They asked, "What game do I want to win?" And then they found the shortest path to influence inside it.

They knew how to turn insight into leverage. How to turn relationships into strategy. How to walk into a room, already owning the outcome. The rules that work aren't about perfection. They're about position. You don't need to know everything. You just need to know what matters and how to frame it.

And the best part? Once you know what rules actually move things, you stop wasting energy on the ones that don't. You become dangerous. Not because you're louder. But because you're clear.

I used to think I'd get what I deserved. If I worked harder, proved myself, and stayed loyal; the results would follow. Respect. Promotion. Wealth. Freedom. But that's not how the world works.

You don't get what you deserve. You get what you negotiate.

And most people never learn to negotiate the rules that matter most, because no one teaches them that they can. We're handed life scripts and told to accept them. The job offer. The salary. The interest rate. The hours. The expectations. The pace. The ladder.

No one tells you that all of it is up for debate. Not just the big stuff. Everything. Your value. Your time. Your future. Your boundaries.

If you're stuck in a job you hate, a relationship that drains you, a life that feels like it belongs to someone else, it's probably not because you failed. It's because somewhere along the line, you accepted terms you didn't even know could be negotiated.

But you can. You can challenge the assumptions. You can ask better questions. You can redraw the map.

So, ask yourself:

- What rules am I following that were never mine?
- What assumptions have I never questioned?
- What room am I in, and what conversation is happening underneath the surface?
- Am I chasing approval, or designing leverage?

The Rules They Never Taught You

Most people see rules as walls. But the people who win? They see them as whiteboards. They erase. They edit. They draft new frameworks entirely. Not because they're special, but because someone showed them how. And now? That someone is you.

This isn't just a book of hacks or high-performance mantras.

It's a set of keys designed to open doors you didn't know were locked. Because once you learn how systems actually work; how capital flows, how influence compounds, how decisions get made behind the scenes, you can stop reacting. And start designing the game you want to play.

You walk into a room differently when you understand the language of power. You ask sharper questions. You stop waiting for permission. You stop playing a game you were never meant to win.

Because now, finally, you see it. Not the illusion. The code. And when you can see the code, you can rewrite the rules.

Because the rules that are shaping the world aren't in policy manuals or mission statements.

They were in side conversations, handshakes, favors, gatekeepers.

Most of them weren't taught, they were enforced. Quietly.

And by the time you noticed, you'd already broken one.

That's the shift. That's the invitation. Not just to escape the trap. But to architect something better. Because the first real rule they never taught you is this:

You're allowed to design the game. You just have to stop playing the one they gave you.

.::. - I didn't lose because I wasn't ready. I lost because I was following rules that were never meant to help me win. The real game was happening beneath the surface.

It's spoken in glances, timing, and unspoken terms.

Power didn't show up with instructions.

It moved quietly, through presence and positioning. And for years, I was fluent in the wrong language. But once I saw the layer, once I stopped chasing fairness and started building leverage, the board shifted.

The real shift isn't learning to play better.

It's realizing you're allowed to change the game.

And the people who do?

They don't wait for the rules.

They write them.

The
Invisible
Framework

The architecture of effort is what determines its reach.

Chapter 3
The Language Of Leverage

*"Leverage is not effort.
It's structure."*

I was 14, working both as a cook and janitor at Burger King when I first heard the phrase "make money in your sleep."

It was a story about Donald Trump. Love him or hate him, the part that stuck with me wasn't about politics or personality. It was math. The article said he made more money in one hour sleeping than I would make in an entire year behind that counter.

I'd come home with grease in my hair and mop water on my shoes. My hands smelled like fryer oil. But something about that line, "money in your sleep," pierced through the noise. It didn't make me angry. It made me curious. It hit differently. Not because I wanted to be a billionaire. But because for the first time, I realized: there were other ways of doing things.

They never taught us about leverage in school. They taught labor. Show up on time. Follow instructions. Trade hours for dollars. Do it again tomorrow.

But real power doesn't come from doing more. It comes from changing what effort means in the first place.

Leverage is the language of builders. Of owners. Of those who understand that one well-placed decision can do more than ten years of hard work. And yet, most people spend their entire lives trading their hours playing by the rules made by everyone else instead of compounding structure.

For years I lived on the wrong side of leverage. I worked for companies that scaled without me. I made other people rich. And I was told to be grateful for the opportunity. It didn't matter how many hours I worked or how perfect I was at my job, because I didn't own any part of the system I was feeding.

Then I built something different.

Not just a hustle. Not just a product. A real system.

I remember pitching the early version over a conference call.

My mentor had invited someone I deeply respected to listen in, a heavyweight in the industry. I walked through the strategy, the framework, the why behind every part.

When I finished, there was a pause. Then the voice came through the speaker. Calm. Certain.

"Congratulations, Renner. You're ready to launch."

That moment stayed with me.

Because for the first time, I wasn't the product.

The system was.

I built the strategy. The framework. The positioning.

Now producers run with it. They leverage my design, and I leverage their reach and knowledge.

That multiplication doesn't start with money. It starts with a mindset.

Pause here.
Do you still see your time as your value?
Or have you started to realize it's just the most expensive way to measure worth?
We all start by trading time. But the moment you question that trade, your blueprint begins to change.

Leverage is not a trick. It's not cheating. It's not reserved for the elite. It's a design principle. And it's available to anyone who stops asking, "How can I do more?" and starts asking, "How can this do more without me?"

Ask yourself:
- What system have I built that works without me?
- What value do I own that others can scale?
- What process can be multiplied through others, technology, capital, or structure?

These are not hypothetical questions. They are design principles. And they change your life the moment you start answering them.

Machines. Teams. Technology. Strategy. Contracts. Consultants. Systems. All of them are forms of multiplication.

All of them turn hours into assets.

For years I asked, "How can I get ahead?" But in every boardroom, in every country, in every government negotiation, the real players were asking a different question: "How can I stop being the bottleneck?"

Most people don't ask these questions because they don't even know they can. But leverage is contagious. You don't need to master it right away. You just need to be around it.

Get in the right rooms. Rooms where people are buying companies instead of asking for raises. Rooms where they build once and sell forever. Where they use capital to buy time instead of trading time for money. Where they ask who they can empower, not what they can personally finish.

Exposure is the real educator. It rewires your brain faster than any course or seminar. I spent years working across government programs in over 80 territories. Each program came with new obstacles. New delays. New rules. And every single time, I had to figure out a way forward, fast. It wasn't just about getting approval. It was about solving real problems. And every solution became another lever I could pull later.

Because that's what leverage really is: Accumulated clarity. Earned fluency. The ability to turn obstacles into operating manuals.

Ask yourself:
- What problem have I solved that others are still struggling with?
- What insight have I earned that could save someone else years?
- What if that became a product?
- What system or solution am I underestimating because it came easy to me?

Take Alex, an independent filmmaker buried in pitch decks and rejection emails. He'd spent years chasing investors for small-budget projects, barely scraping by.

We reframed one of his workflows into a repeatable pitch package others could use. Within weeks, he had a second income stream and producers were calling him to consult on their projects.

He didn't work harder. He designed smarter.

Then there was Marcus, a business owner juggling three companies like live grenades. Burnt out. Always on. Always behind.

We restructured his week: two days building systems, one day onboarding help, the rest focused on refinement. Within six months, he was out of the weeds, and his revenue jumped 40%.

Leverage doesn't always look like some brilliant invention.

Sometimes it's just the decision to stop repeating something manually and start teaching it.

Ask yourself:

- Where am I currently the bottleneck?
- What task or routine is draining my time but not building value?
- What would my income look like if 80% of it came from systems?

Be honest with yourself.

Are you holding onto it because no one else can do it... or because you need to feel needed?

Once you see what leverage looks like, you stop asking for permission. You start designing systems that scale without you.

You don't need to have it all figured out. You just need to decide that you're done playing on the wrong side of leverage. Stop trading hours. Start designing multipliers.

Everything you want becomes easier when you stop doing it all yourself. And this? This is where the climb actually begins.

You're not building a business. You're building a system that frees you.

Because leverage is the sword in the stone. The thing you couldn't lift, until now.

Ask yourself:
- Where am I still being heroic instead of being strategic?
- What would my world look like if everything ran 20% better without me?
- What version of my work would still function if I disappeared for a month?

And once that clicks? You'll never see the world the same way again.

Leverage isn't just about output. It's about perspective. It's seeing your value not as a person who performs, but as a person who designs performance into systems, people, and processes.

And the real truth? Leverage is ethical. It's not stepping on others to get ahead. It's building ladders so more can climb. It's recognizing that your greatest contribution isn't how hard you work, but how well you build.

So, the question is no longer, "How much can I do?"

The question is:

"What can I build that does more... even when I rest?"

Because leverage is the sword in the stone.

The thing you couldn't lift, until now.

Not because you weren't strong.

But because you finally stopped pulling,

and started designing the hand that lifts.

.::. - I didn't grow up around systems. I grew up around sweat.

Effort was how you proved your worth. But the older I got, the more I saw something else, something invisible running in the background of every success story.

Leverage.
Not luck.
Not inheritance.
Structure.

I used to believe I had to do it all myself. That if I worked hard enough, I'd eventually earn freedom. But freedom doesn't come from effort alone. It comes from how you structure effort. From what you own, what you build, and what works without you.

That's when it all changed. I stopped asking how much I could carry. And started asking how far this could run without me.

Leverage isn't about stepping back. It's about stepping up, into the role of designer, builder, multiplier.

It's not ease.
It's impact.
It's the moment you stop being the engine...
and become the architect.

The
Mountain Path

*Build what's worth climbing.
Leave behind what isn't.*

Chapter 4
Designing The Mountain

*"Design the mountain you're willing to climb.
Then build the path to reach the top."*

For a long time, I didn't know what I was building. I just knew I didn't want to stay where I was. I tried door-to-door sales. Credit card sales rep. Construction. Website designer. Government economic and jobs programs. Anything that offered a chance to climb, without realizing I was still climbing someone else's mountain.

It wasn't failure. It was movement. But it wasn't movement with direction.

Then I got thrown into the deep end.

I stared at the task like it was a prank.

No team. No support. Just an email and a deadline.

For a moment, I sat frozen, staring out the window thinking:

Who am I to lead this?

But that voice, the one that doubts, only wins if it becomes louder than your mission.

I was tasked with building a legislative green light committee for a new government initiative, something that had never been done before. To move the program forward, I had to gather a coalition of the most respected minds in tech, finance, media, and policy, and get them all to sit at the same table under my leadership.

No title. No budget. No precedent. Just a deadline, a rough idea, and my voice.

I remember sitting in my office that day, scribbling names on a notepad. Not the safe picks. The real ones. The kind of people who rarely returned calls from people like me. But I made the calls anyway. I made the case, not for myself, but for the impact. For what this could mean for their legacy, their industries, their communities.

A few said no.

But many said yes.

And that committee didn't just move a program forward. It moved me forward. It became the moment I realized: I didn't have to climb someone else's mountain. I could build my own.

That was the real shift.

Clarity doesn't come all at once. It builds. It sharpens with every obstacle. Government work gave me the best education I never paid for. Every program came with new barriers: legal, political, cultural. And every time, I had to create a path through.

That path became the blueprint. It taught me that strategy isn't a luxury. It's survival.

I stopped asking, "What job should I do?" and started asking, "What system do I want to live inside?"

That's when ownership begins. Not when you get the perfect title. But when you stop asking for someone else's permission to climb.

It's easy to confuse motion with progress. I chased a lot of things early on that looked impressive from the outside; job titles, partnerships, contracts with logos people recognized. But somewhere along the way, I realized: I wasn't moving toward my mountain. I was climbing someone else's.

Pause here.
Have you ever climbed hard toward a goal, only to realize it wasn't even yours?
That you were chasing someone else's version of success?
That moment isn't failure.
It's your signal.
Not to stop climbing, but to choose a better mountain.

False summits are dangerous. They exhaust you. You reach what you think is the top, only to realize it was just a marketing platform for someone else's goal. The real climb hadn't even started yet.

That's when I started designing.

Design isn't about control. It's about alignment. I began crafting my days differently. Making decisions not by how impressive they looked on paper, but by whether they moved me closer to the real summit.

And I let people go. Not out of anger. But out of truth.

One of them was a close friend I'd brought into several deals.

We shared vision, but not discipline. I kept waiting for him to rise with me. He didn't.

Letting go wasn't loud. No fallout. Just a quiet decision to stop forcing the fit.

And the air got lighter afterward.

Some people aren't meant for your mountain. Some are amazing, just not aligned. Others may have been right for one season but can't handle the altitude where you're going. Letting them go isn't a failure. It's focus.

Ask yourself:
- Whose mountain am I climbing?
- Who in my circle is resisting the altitude?
- What distractions have I mistaken for milestones?

Vision sharpens under pressure. The more resistance I faced, the more I had to build clarity or break under the weight. And each round of pressure gave me better tools. Not just systems. But standards.

I learned to build with the end in mind. Not for vanity. Not for applause. But for alignment. I learned to let go of perfect and start chasing real.

Momentum followed. Not overnight. But piece by piece.

Because once you start building the right mountain, the one that's yours, the terrain changes. Obstacles don't stop you. They sharpen you.

You feel pulled forward. Not pushed around.

And then it happens. One day, someone else follows your path.

Not because you asked them to. But because they saw clarity in your direction. They felt something solid in the way you climb. Sometimes they reach out years later. Sometimes it's just a glance across a table, or a quiet DM that says, "You changed how I think."

And in that moment, you realize:

You didn't just design the mountain.

You became it.

.::. - I spent years climbing, until I realized I never asked where the mountain was taking me.

I said yes to opportunities that looked good on paper. I chased progress without questioning the destination. I moved up... but not forward. I was gaining altitude on someone else's map.

The turning point didn't feel like a breakthrough. It felt like a burden. A project with no support. A deadline with no roadmap.

And a question I couldn't shake: 'Who am I to lead this?'

But buried in the chaos was clarity.

Not because I had it all figured out.

But because I finally stopped waiting for someone else's path to make sense.

That's when the real work began:

Designing a mountain that was mine.

One aligned with my values, my vision, and my capacity to carry others up with me.

It wasn't about building faster. It was about building on purpose.

Letting go of the wrong climbers. Choosing direction over decoration.

And learning that clarity doesn't come at the top, it's earned with every disciplined step.

Because eventually, if you design it well enough, someone else will climb because of the path you left behind.

The
First Light

Where conviction walks ahead of proof.

CHAPTER 5
BUILDING IN THE DARK

*"Before there were frameworks,
there were post-its.
Before there were allies,
there was just belief."*

The beginning is never clean.
No welcome party. No media buzz. No master plan.
Just a late night, a notebook, and a vision too loud to ignore.
I remember the early days, not the first spark, but the fog that came after. When the idea had chosen me, but nothing around me confirmed it was real.
I still clearly remember that night in the FedEx parking lot, under the cold glare of streetlights, holding mockups nobody requested. I stared blankly at my hands gripping

the steering wheel, my knuckles white, palms sweaty, whispering into the silence: 'Am I losing it?'

Silence hung in the car, heavy and unkind. Then a quiet voice, my own and not my own, came back softly: 'Maybe. But you can't stop now.'

No office. No team. No traction. Just the ache to build and the chaos that came with it.

This is the mountain no one trains you for.

The idea stage.

The spreadsheet-in-your-head stage.

The "I know this sounds crazy but just hear me out" stage.

I started with nothing but conviction. I couldn't pay salaries. I couldn't guarantee outcomes. All I had were mindshots of logos that didn't exist yet and ideas that made sense in 3 a.m. monologues. And yet, somehow, a few people said yes. Not to the plan. To the person.

They weren't co-founders. Not yet. They were believers. Sometimes skeptical. Sometimes unsure. But present. They stuck around even when the hours were long, and the idea was more mess than map.

Pause here.
Remember the moment you almost quit?
When no one saw it but you,
and belief felt heavier than progress?
That wasn't failure.
That was foundation.
What you're building isn't fragile.
It's just early.

We didn't have departments. We had "whoever's free." Everyone did everything. Sales one day. Product the next. Legal in the morning, lunch at the local coffee shop, then a napkin pitch to a potential investor over pizza that night.

There were no role descriptions, just problems looking for hands.
And still... it moved.
Slowly. Badly. Awkwardly.
But it moved.
That movement came with weight. Because in this phase, every win feels bigger than it is. Every setback feels fatal. You're one email away from breakthrough, and one distraction away from collapse. The perpetual two weeks away from getting paid.

I remember one afternoon we didn't have money for proper software licenses. We stitched together a product from free trials, borrowed time, and the kind of grit you can't fake. Another time, we couldn't afford business cards, so I printed a single copy and laminated it to keep showing the same one to people. It was ridiculous. But it worked.

This is the part no one sees. The blurry, duct-taped, barely-holding-together part. The emotional overdraft you run every single day. The unspoken panic you swallow just to get through one more pitch, one more meeting, one more round of "what do you actually do?"

And yet... this is where the DNA forms.

You learn to listen differently. To stretch trust. To build on fog.

You discover who shows up when there's no spotlight. Who leans in without needing credit. Who asks hard questions instead of just nodding. That's when you realize: not everyone around you is a builder. Some are just borrowing belief.

It took me a while to tell the difference.

Some early team members were electric. Full of ideas. Loud in meetings. High energy.

Jake was like that. First to raise his hand. Big vision. Big personality. But when timelines slipped, so did he. When the pressure came, he started dodging decisions, stirring friction, blaming others.

He didn't want clarity. Because clarity removed the illusion of control.

Then there was Lila. Quieter. Less polished. Sharp-eyed. She didn't pitch much, but she caught every dropped ball. No noise. No ego. Just presence. When storms hit, she filled gaps without being asked. She didn't orbit me. She anchored the mission.

That's when I started to understand:

Not everyone around you is a builder.

Some are just borrowing belief.

In this phase, you'll be tempted to hold onto everyone. Every hand feels necessary. Every contributor feels irreplaceable. But that's not loyalty. That's fear.

The truth is, some people aren't meant to scale with you. And that's okay.

This is the season to observe. Not just who shows up, but who makes things better. Who takes initiative without being asked. Who sees the gaps and doesn't wait to be assigned. Because the team you build here won't just define your momentum. They'll define your culture.

Ask yourself:

- Who carries with me?
- Who waits for me?
- Who resists the clarity I'm starting to build?

There's a difference between co-visionaries and co-dependents.

Between allies and attachments. Between energy and alignment.

I learned that by failing. I trusted too fast. Gave access without criteria. Let enthusiasm replace discernment. And when pressure hit, the cracks showed.

One day, after a brutal week of misfires and miscommunication, I wasn't just questioning the team. I was questioning the whole thing. Whether I could keep going. Whether it was even worth salvaging. I had poured everything into the vision... but I couldn't carry dead weight anymore. I sat in the car outside our workspace and asked myself the question I'd been avoiding: "If I had to start again tomorrow, who would I bring with me?"

That question broke me. Then it built me.

Because I wasn't just pruning the team. I was pruning myself.

Because the truth is, the beginning is not just about building the thing. It's about building the builders. And that means learning how to lead in the dark, when your voice still trembles, when your idea still feels fragile, when your own belief is the only thing louder than your fear.

But that's where the real leaders are forged. Not in spotlight. In silhouette. When the vision hasn't been validated yet. When the team doesn't see the mountain, just the map you're drawing in real time.

And if you can lead then, when it's messy, unpaid, uncertain?

You'll carry something most leaders never earn:

Conviction rooted in chaos.

Clarity born from fog.

And the kind of culture that doesn't depend on momentum... because it was built without it.

So if you're still there, in the fog, in the building phase, in the barely-making-rent scramble, I want you to hear this:

You're not behind.

You're not broken.

You're in the fire that forges architects.

And what you're building...

It's not fragile.

Building In The Dark

It's just early.
Keep going.
Because the ones who build in the dark?
They don't just find the light.
They become it.

.::. - You don't always know when it begins. There's no grand opening. No ribbon to cut. Just a restless night, a half-formed idea, and a kind of madness that whispers, keep going.

You build before you're ready.

You speak before you're sure.

And somehow, the vision pulls people in.

Not because it's clear, but because you are.

In the dark, you learn who will carry weight, and who will become it. You find your rhythm in the fog. Your real allies don't orbit, they anchor.

And slowly, painfully, something starts to form. A culture. A cadence. A clarity. Not loud, but unmistakable.

You aren't just building a product. You're becoming the proof.

Not because you had the answers. But because you refused to let the silence be louder than the mission.

That's how real companies are born.

That's how real leaders are forged.

In the dark, where most never look long enough to see the shape of the light.

The
Shifting Crew

Not everyone climbs.
Some just hold the rope...
to slow you down.

CHAPTER 6
TESTS AND ALLIES

*"The climb reveals who's climbing with you...
and who's holding onto your rope."*

Every vision eventually gets tested, not just by the world, but by the people around you.

This is where it gets real.

Designing the mountain is one thing. Climbing it? That's where the real tests begin.

The moment you take your vision public, two things happen:

You attract attention. You trigger resistance.

People begin to circle around you: some to help, some to watch, some to sabotage. And often, you can't tell who's who until the weather turns. When the path is steep and the air gets thin, the wrong team becomes a liability. And the cost of carrying the wrong people isn't just delay, it's disaster.

I learned that the hard way.

There was a time I believed loyalty was enough. That if I trusted people, empowered them, gave them access, they would treat that access with integrity. I thought shared vision meant shared values.

I believed the right people would rise with me if I gave them enough trust.

So I gave them everything.

Then came the project. $5.5 billion. A multi-use plaza unlike anything before.

The plaza wasn't just another development; it was a blueprint for what cities could become. It was designed to create thousands of jobs, bring advanced education and workforce training to underserved communities, and spark innovation through modern infrastructure. It had the potential to uplift an entire region, not just economically, but socially.

I had done the heavy lifting.

Secured government support.

Built the strategy.

Lined up financial partners.

Brought in real collaborators.

The foundation was solid. The momentum was real. The future looked bright.

But then came the fracture, when their greed boiled over, their lack of vision exposed their emptiness, and their true nature, selfish, deceitful, and small, finally showed itself.

Some of the early team, people I had trusted, mentored, and given real opportunities to, began operating in the shadows.

They didn't just talk. They moved.

They cut side deals behind my back.

They interfered directly with the land purchase offer, introducing confusion and delays that damaged trust and stalled negotiations.

And then, in a move that exposed everything, they circumvented my company's formal offer and submitted their own, in their own name, attempting to seize the land and the project for themselves.

They claimed credit for work they didn't do. Made decisions they weren't authorized to make. They used my name and my project to chase their own agendas, and when that wasn't enough, they slandered me to partners and government officials, discredited my reputation, and made personal threats.

And when they realized they couldn't control the vision, they took it by force, through manipulation, false claims, and legal deception.

What followed was a mess.

A tangle of betrayals, interference, and lawsuits.

And the project?

It stalled.

Despite everything it could have become, despite the jobs, the schools, the infrastructure, it hasn't moved forward since.

A vision that once promised so much, held hostage by the very people who were supposed to help it rise.

It was betrayal with a smile. And for a moment, it shook me.

Because when the people you believed in cut you out of your own vision, it doesn't just hurt. It makes you question your judgment. Your leadership. Your instinct. I went back through every meeting in my head, wondering what I missed. What signs I ignored. What boundaries I never set.

But I didn't fold.

I stepped back. Assessed. Documented. Rebuilt. Not only because I wanted revenge. But because I had clarity.

Clarity that this wasn't just about a project. It was about designing a future where that kind of sabotage couldn't happen again.

So, I restructured everything. Legal frameworks. Internal controls. Partnership criteria. I stopped looking for people who clapped for me and started searching for people who could carry with me.

Because allies don't need credit. They want progress. Ask yourself:
- Who has proven they can stay steady when the pressure hits?
- Who are you trusting out of convenience, not conviction?
- Who multiplies your vision instead of just orbiting it?

Pause Here
When did you first notice someone was pulling your climb off course?
Not because they said no,
but because they said yes and didn't mean it.
We all have that moment.
Not when the plan failed.
But when the people did.
That's not the fall.
That's the filter.

Some people aren't teammates. They're tourists or even worse, thieves. They stop by for the view but never carry weight on the trail. And when the weather changes, tourists don't pull you up, they pull you down.

And you? You're too busy surviving to realize you're dragging dead weight.

One of my closest allies today started as a quiet presence in early meetings, asking smart and challenging questions. He never spoke just to be heard. But when the pressure hit, he moved. He filled gaps. He took hits I didn't see coming. Not for applause. For mission.

That's when I knew he was more than support. He was infrastructure.

The climb strips away illusion. Some people say they're with you, but what they really mean is: as long as it's easy. As long as there's applause. As long as you don't outgrow them.

Some build with you. Others copy you. Some say they have your back. But they're really just scouting for weakness. Some smile in photos. Then whisper doubts in private.

Ask yourself:
- Who shows up when it's quiet?
- Who keeps showing up when it's hard?
- Who are you protecting that hasn't protected you back?

The truth is: none of this means you're on the wrong path. It means you're finally on the real one. The one that filters for alignment.

Tests don't just expose flaws in your plan. They expose fractures in your circle. That's when refinement becomes non-negotiable. You stop chasing unity. You start building alignment. You stop hiring hope. You start recruiting discipline.

Ask yourself:
- If I had to rebuild today, who do I invite again?
- What role needs redefining?
- What partnership should I look at again?

You won't always see betrayal coming, but now you can design your own system, so betrayal loses its power over you. Your real allies will answer the call without needing to be asked. They don't need a spotlight. They just need clarity.

And when you find them? Hold them tight. Everyone else? Let the mountain sort them.

Because the climb doesn't just change your view. It changes your crew.

And that's not a loss. That's the price of elevation.

You don't just get tested. You get tempered, like steel, shaped by fire. Stronger. Sharper. Built to last through more than just applause.

You stop being someone who joins big things. And start being someone who builds them.

I didn't just rebuild my trust. I rebuilt my blueprint.

Because at the end of the day, you don't just climb the mountain.

You become it.

.::. - Betrayal doesn't show up in a villain's cape. It comes with a smile and a handshake.
And when it hits, it cuts deeper than failure ever could.
Because it came from someone you let in.
But here's the truth no one tells you: the fall is a filter.
It clears the fog. It sharpens your view. It reveals who's for the vision, and who's just along for the visibility.
You don't need applause. You need alignment.
You don't need loyalty in name. You need loyalty in weight.
Because the climb gets steep. And the ones who stay? They don't just stand with you.
They build with you.
And when the storm clears, they're still there...
not for credit, but for legacy.

The
Furnace

Where conviction is melted, and clarity is forged.

Chapter 7
The Ordeal

*"The fall doesn't define you.
What you do after does."*

    This is the part no one prepares you for.
    The sleepless nights. The unanswered calls. The moment when everything you've worked for vanishes, not because it wasn't good enough, but because the wrong detail slipped, the wrong pressure hit, or the wrong person cracked at the wrong time.
    This is where the Journey stops being metaphor and starts being real.
    There's one night I'll never forget, parked behind that 24-hour gym, the cold seeping through my jacket and breath fogging up the car windows. My car wasn't transportation anymore; it was shelter. I'd lost everything... again. No safe place to sleep, account balance

The Ordeal

at zero, and the last call I had was with the bank, coldly warning me they'd soon seize the little I had left.

Sitting there, shivering, it wasn't just desperation; it was disbelief. How did I end up here again? Yet beneath the numbness, a stubborn whisper reminded me, almost defiant: 'This isn't how your story ends.'

I sat in the dark, phone on 2% battery, holding a notebook full of big ideas that now felt like broken ideas. That moment wasn't cinematic. It was raw. Desperate. The kind of night that strips you of illusion. I cried hard. When I stopped, I started planning again. Not because I believed I could still win. But because I had nothing left to lose. And that, oddly, was the beginning of power. Not inspiring. Not Instagrammable. Just real.

I've had more than one moment that nearly broke me. I've been homeless, sleeping in my car; not once, but three separate times. I've filed bankruptcy twice. I've watched businesses implode overnight because of mistakes I didn't know I was making. One of the most painful? Commingling the company's and my personal bank accounts to help cover for the underperforming company. It felt small. It wasn't. It was the loose thread that unraveled everything.

That shortcut turned into a sinkhole. I thought I was saving time, avoiding red tape. But when things got tight and questions started coming, investors, accountants, even vendors. I found myself saying, "I think," "I guess," "Maybe." And that was the tell. If you don't know, you don't lead. That moment taught me a hard rule I follow to this day: if your answer starts with uncertainty, you're not ready. Get clear... or don't move.

But none of those were the end. They were thresholds.

Here's what no one tells you: Those moments don't mean you're not worthy. They mean you're being forged.

The collapse of a visual effects company I built hit the hardest. I remember sitting in the office that morning, the silence louder than any argument. Desks empty. Phones unplugged. A whiteboard still full of plans that would never happen. My lead designer left a note on my desk. That was the moment it felt real.

Not the drained accounts. Not the client cancellations. It was the absence. The weight of something that had once pulsed with life now sitting still. I turned off the lights, locked the door, and walked out not just of a business, but of an era I thought would define me. It wasn't just the money. It was identity. I had tied so much of who I was to the team, the reputation, the success. And when it crumbled, I didn't just lose income. I lost meaning. I couldn't speak about it for months. It felt like erasure.

But that collapse? It was also a release. That business wasn't aligned. It brought freedom, applause, and distraction. But not direction. And deep down, I knew it. It took a fire to make me admit it.

I stopped asking, "How do I rebuild what I lost?" and started asking, "What do I want to build now that I know better?"

Ask yourself:
- What failure are you still holding onto as proof you shouldn't try again?
- What part of you needs to die so your next level can live?

After the wreckage, I started to reconstruct everything. Not just the business. The principles. The foundation. I learned that if you want to build something lasting, you need more than vision; you need infrastructure. And at the core of that infrastructure is risk mitigation. Every structure I build, even the routines in my personal life, is rooted in anticipating risk, absorbing impact, and creating systems that protect against the unexpected. Because success without safeguards is just a countdown to collapse.

It started with structure. I stopped trusting memory and built playbooks. Documented workflows. Created protocols. Because if your business depends on personality, memory, or hope, it's not a business. It's a liability.

That's why I now build every venture like a vault. Layered protections. Emergency protocols. Multiple redundancies. Because no matter how good the plan is, what matters most is how it holds when things go wrong.

One of the most dangerous habits I had to break was answering questions with words like "I think," "maybe," or "I guess." Those aren't strategies, they're stall-outs. If you don't know the answer, you better find it before you move forward. Because uncertainty at the top creates chaos everywhere else. Clients can feel it. Teams get confused by it. Plans fall apart under it. That's a lesson the collapse of the visual effects company burned into me. I didn't just lose money, I lost trust, because I didn't have clear, confident answers when they mattered most.

Pause Here.
The fall doesn't announce itself.
It just... arrives. Quiet. Brutal. Clarifying.
But this isn't about endings.
It's about what survives.
If you're in it right now, the unraveling, the silence, the self-doubt. Don't panic.
You're not broken. You're being redesigned.
Not for perfection.
For permanence.

If you're not aligned, if you don't have a known path, a defined decision, a documented truth; then you're gambling, not building.

It continued with people. I stopped hiring based on loyalty and started hiring for capability. Gave equity to performance, not enthusiasm. And when the pressure came again, the right ones stood up. They didn't need hand-holding. They needed a mission.

And it finished with standards. I confronted friction fast.

Missed deadlines. Vague roles. Unspoken expectations. All of it.

Because I learned: small problems grow teeth. Left unchecked, they devour clarity, culture, and trust.

Ask yourself:
- What standard have you been tolerating that keeps tripping your momentum?
- What system do you need to build to protect your progress from your past?

You've heard this part already.

The empty desks. The sticky note. The silence louder than failure.

But at the time, I only saw loss. What I didn't see, what I couldn't see, was the pattern.

The fragile infrastructure. The invisible risks. The lack of redundancy.

That wasn't just a collapse; it was a case study I hadn't written yet.

That moment didn't just hurt, it taught.

And what it taught became the foundation for everything I now call risk mitigation.

There was a Tuesday, regular in every way, where I noticed a payment had bounced. I was in the middle of drafting an investor update when the notification flashed across my screen: "Payment declined." I stared at it, confused. I double-checked the bank portal. Not only had the payment failed, but two others had been reversed, and the account was unexpectedly overdrawn.

That was the first tremor. I picked up the phone to call the finance lead, no answer. Then the operations manager. Voicemail.

I walked out to the office floor. Same desks. Same note. But this time, I saw the architecture behind the silence, the weak systems, the ignored red flags, the lack of safeguards.

It wasn't just a collapse. It was the consequence of compromises I hadn't tracked and shortcuts I hadn't labeled as such.

And now it was all visible.

The silence in that moment was deafening. It wasn't just a missed payment. It was the collapse made visible. It was the exact second the illusion broke. And I remember thinking: "This is how it ends? Not with a bang, but with a bounce and a silence?"

I sat in that silence for a long time. I replayed every missed cue. Every ignored red flag. Every compromise I made in the name of speed. And then I opened a blank document titled: 'Next Time.' That file became a 37-page protocol built on principles I still use today. New clients hadn't signed. Bank records made no sense. I was too late. The cracks had started long before. And I was still telling myself the story that it would turn around.

But this time, I didn't just watch it collapse. I documented the pattern. I dissected it. And then I designed a future where that pattern couldn't repeat.

Risk mitigation isn't about playing scared, it's about building smart. It's the discipline of asking, "What could break?" and designing around it before it ever does. It's how I lead now. Not by assuming the best, but by preparing for the worst, and making sure we can still win anyway.

Because leaders don't survive storms. They architect through them.

The deeper I went, the clearer I became. The story I had been telling myself; that if I failed, I wasn't good enough, wasn't true. What was true? I was playing too small. Too reactionary. Too alone.

Everything changed when I started seeing failure as friction that sharpens; an early warning system for better design, not just a bruise to recover from. From that moment forward, I began writing new rules: debrief every setback, document every decision chain, and flag moments when emotion drives action. These micro-policies helped turn trauma into training, and gave me something failure alone never could, structure. Not a sign to stop, but a signal to pivot.

Now, before any big initiative, I run what I call a "Conviction Audit." I ask: Do I know this, or do I feel it? Am I hoping... or planning? If I say "I think," I pause. Because "I think" is a stall, not a strategy. That small shift has saved me millions.

One night, after the collapse, I sat in a coffee shop with nothing but a laptop and a cup of coffee I couldn't afford. I wrote down three columns: "What I know now," "What I would never do again," and "What I still believe in." That exercise became the blueprint for everything I've built since.

I began creating a Failure Map, a simple framework I still use today. Every failure has a pattern. If you study it, you can spot the weak signals before they get loud. You can build stronger.

Ask yourself:
- What did your last failure teach you that success never could?
- What are you pretending not to see right now?
- What fear are you mistaking for wisdom?

You won't feel ready. You won't feel strong. But you will be forged. And when you come through the fire, you'll carry something stronger than confidence.

You'll carry clarity.

And clarity builds empires.

Because what you build next…

Won't be built on fear.

It'll be built on fire.

.::. - I used to think failure meant the end.
But the truth is, it's the forge.
Where illusions burn off. Where shortcuts collapse. Where unearned clarity dies.
That season behind the gym? In the parked car? That wasn't the end of my story.
It was the crucible.
Because when everything else was stripped away,
I found what couldn't be taken:
Conviction.
And from that came clarity.
And from that? Infrastructure.
Now I don't build for speed.
I build for resilience.
For seasons I haven't met yet.
For storms that don't make the headlines but test everything behind the scenes.
What you build after the fire isn't fragile.
It's forged.
Because the ones who keep building after the fall?
They don't just rise again.
They design higher ground.

The
Forge

*Where fire stops being a test,
and becomes the tool.*

Chapter 8
The Reward

*"You don't need to conquer the world.
You just need to reclaim your place in it."*

This is when you know the fire didn't burn you. It forged you.

Something shifts, not outside, but inside. The doubt that once roared becomes quiet. The hesitation that made you flinch now sharpens your edge. You begin to move differently. Not louder. Just clearer. With conviction not born from hype, but from scars.

You stop micromanaging conversations in your head. You don't shrink to fit the room. You stop performing strength and start embodying it. And even in uncertainty, you carry certainty, not because the future is known, but because you've learned to hold the unknown without panic.

The Reward

You don't wake up with a parade. There's no thunderclap announcing your growth. It happens between breaths; when you stop apologizing for your pace, when you stop second-guessing your seat at the table. You notice the tension leaves your shoulders. You speak without rehearsing. You make a decision and don't immediately seek approval. That's the real shift. It's not arrival. It's return. To yourself.

After the betrayals, the silence, the collapse of things that once defined me, I didn't find glory.

I found something better: command.

Not over others. Over myself. There was a moment, quiet and small, but unforgettable. I was sitting alone at my desk, papers spread out, ideas flowing. No team. No applause. No one to impress. I looked up, and it hit me: I wasn't asking for permission anymore. Not to speak. Not to build. Not to lead.

There was a coffee mug on the corner of the desk. My pen had run dry. I was running on fumes, but I wasn't afraid. I didn't need a vote. I needed a plan. That's when I realized: conviction doesn't arrive with fanfare. It shows up when you've lost too much to pretend anymore.

It felt like a quiet graduation. A release from every meeting where I'd once minimized my voice. Every pitch where I'd watered down the truth just to stay in the room. That moment wasn't loud, but it echoed. It said, "This is yours now. Act like it."

That was the real reward.

Not safety. Not certainty. Command. The kind that doesn't flinch in storms because it was born inside one. The kind that stops chasing noise and starts building signals.

And this is where the story shifts.

When you stop reacting. When you stop negotiating with people who haven't earned the right to shape your vision. When you no longer tolerate friction disguised as friendship, or sabotage disguised as support.

Leadership isn't something you grow into. It's something you reclaim.

After the visual effects company fell apart, I went quiet. I didn't need advice. I needed alignment. I had to rebuild from the ground up, not just with tools and spreadsheets, but with a philosophy. A risk-mitigation mindset. One where every structure I created; every contract, every company, every conversation, was filtered through the same lens: Does this reduce exposure? Does this preserve clarity? Does this create traction without fragility?

I started applying what I now call "The 4-R Filter": Resilience, Redundancy, Role clarity, and Real-time response. Every decision passed through it. If a plan couldn't hold during volatility, if a team didn't know their precise weight, if a system couldn't course-correct on contact, I redesigned it.

Risk wasn't the enemy. Unexamined risk was.

I began asking better questions: What's the worst-case scenario? Can this survive betrayal? Delay? Legal scrutiny? Emotional fatigue? If the answer wasn't yes across the board, I didn't move forward. Because leadership, I learned, isn't about momentum. It's about insulation. You don't build fast, you build buffered.

That's when I stopped building products. And started building permanence.

It began with a risk mitigated financing vehicle and became a fortress. Strategy became architecture. Risk wasn't just avoided, it was integrated; anticipated, absorbed, neutralized. I didn't want to build something exciting. I wanted to build something unshakable. And the only way to do that was by baking risk mitigation into the DNA of every system.

Then came the product that shook an entire industry. It wasn't just a protective measure. It was a refusal to accept fragility as fate. If the world was going to keep throwing storms, we were going to build with drainage. Shielding people and capital, not with promises, but with protocols. And suddenly I wasn't alone in the vision anymore. The right people found it. They saw not just the mission, but the design.

Alignment began replacing effort. People stopped asking, "What are you trying to do?" and started asking, "How can we make it stronger?"

That's when I knew the reward had landed.

It wasn't loud. It wasn't flashy. It came in the form of traction. Stability. Control. Real allies emerged, not tourists stopping by for the view, but teammates carrying weight on the trail. They weren't seduced by the hype. They were attracted to the infrastructure. The clarity. The lack of chaos. They didn't need attention. They wanted outcomes.

They didn't panic at pressure. They didn't hover when things looked uncertain. And they didn't resurface just to ask how things were going. Real allies don't orbit your potential, they build within it. They don't ask for your spotlight. They bring tools.

Pause Here.
Don't rush past this.
You've felt the heat.
You've carried the climb.
And now, the reward isn't applause.
It's clarity.
It's command.
It's knowing what you're building can actually hold you. Stop and ask yourself:
- What part of my vision finally feels like mine?
- Where am I no longer reacting, but refining?

- Who's showing up to build with me now that I'm not performing?

> You're not just growing.
> You're grounding.
> This is where the scaffolding becomes structure.

One partner called me after reading a memo I'd written. He didn't ask about profits. He asked about sustainability. That's when I knew: this wasn't a hype-chaser. This was someone who saw the weight in the wiring. Someone who understood that true growth isn't loud, it's repeatable.

If you're wondering whether you've crossed that threshold, try this: look at your calendar. How many meetings are defense? How many are design? Then look at your conversations. Are you pitching... or refining? Are you explaining... or executing?

And through all this, I started living differently.

I no longer held space for people who didn't hold weight. I didn't chase clients. I filtered them. I didn't sell vision. I structured it. The applause wasn't needed anymore. Because the work was the reward.

The real wealth was never the money. It was being able to walk into any room, at any time, with no script and no pitch, and still lead the conversation because I was no longer performing. I was placed. Grounded. Clear.

Ask yourself:

- What structure in your life is still built on hope instead of strategy?
- Who still has access to your plans but hasn't earned your trust?
- What would change if you saw risk not as a threat, but as a design signal?

The Reward

The truth is, the fire always comes. But when your foundation is built with foresight, not fear, you stop dreading the fall. You start designing for the rise.

You don't need to conquer the world. Just reclaim your place in it. With tools that last. With partners who carry. With systems that hold.

And once that happens?

You don't just get the reward.

You embody it. You operationalize it. And others begin to orbit not around your ambition, but around your clarity.

That's when you know: You didn't just survive the fire. You designed within it. You shaped steel from heat and structure from hurt. You stopped being the spark. You became the forge.

And now, others don't follow your flame. They're building with your blueprint.

.::. - You'll know you're entering the reward,
not when everything gets easier,
but when everything gets quieter.
When rooms don't shake you.
When doubt no longer decides your voice.
When you can lose a deal and not lose yourself.
That's the shift.
That's the moment you realize: the forge didn't take from you.
It made you.
This isn't the end of the journey.
But it's the moment you stop proving...
and start leading.
You used to chase rooms. Now you build them.
You used to pitch plans. Now people follow your process.
You used to ask, "Am I ready?"
Now you ask, "Is it aligned?"
Because when the vision is real,
when the foundation is earned,
you stop climbing to be seen...
and start rising because you're built to carry others too.

The
Return

*Where the world still sees who you were,
but you now move as who you've become.*

Chapter 9
The Road Back

"When clarity returns louder than applause."

The world doesn't throw a parade just because you changed.

That's the first lesson. After everything; the fire, the failure, the forge, I stepped back into the world not as who I had been, but as who I had become. Sharper. Quieter. More dangerous in the best way. But the world? It didn't notice. Not at first.

You've outgrown your past, but the world hasn't updated its map. Clients still treat you like the rookie you once were. Family still expects you to play small. Even your calendar, your wardrobe, your inbox, they all pull at the version of you that no longer fits.

They still asked me to justify my vision. They still measured me against who I used to be. They still tested me. Only now, I didn't break. I bent. Adjusted. Realigned. But I didn't shatter. Not again. That's the road back: not a walk of shame, but a path of reintegration. You've changed. Now you have to lead like it.

The pressure didn't disappear; it just evolved. In the beginning, I felt pressure to prove I was worth betting on. Later, the pressure came from a different place: protecting what I'd built, strengthening what I had created. I wasn't making decisions for myself anymore. I was deciding for entire families, for international partners, for communities who believed in the blueprint we'd laid down.

I remember sitting at the head of the table during a massive funding meeting. The energy was electric. Valuation numbers were on the whiteboard. The lawyers were ready. All I had to do was say yes. But I paused. Something felt off. Their pitch was polished, but their posture was possessive. They didn't care about the mission, only the multiple. They wanted to own the narrative, reshape the culture, repackage what we'd built.

I remembered every sleepless night. Every no. Every time I scraped together payroll by sheer will. The number on that whiteboard could've erased all of it. But the cost was everything I'd built to protect. I looked around the room. Suits. Smiles. Nothing but extraction in their eyes. Old me would've taken the deal. The new me didn't even hesitate. I closed the folder and said, "If you want the returns, you have to respect the mission."

We walked out without money. But we kept the mission. That decision defined us more than any funding round ever could. What stuck with me wasn't just the money we declined, it was the message we sent. That clarity is now the standard we scale by.

The past has a way of circling back when you're finally in motion.

One day I found myself on a rooftop in LA, face to face with a former partner who'd gone silent the moment things got hard.

Sunlight reflected off the buildings around us. A breeze carried the distant hum of the city. He was all smiles now, the kind of smile that tries to rewrite history.

But I remembered what he'd done.

He was a partner on a film. I gave him real ownership, real opportunity. And he used it to cut side deals I didn't know about.

He got paid. Quietly. Privately. And then he vanished.

No follow-up. No accountability. No delivery.

Just gone.

Leaving me, as one of the actual responsible owners, to make good on his commitments, to fix what he broke and finish what he left behind.

Now here he was again.

Grinning. Polished.

Telling me how proud he was.

Telling me I'd inspired him.

Telling me he wanted back in.

But I remembered the silence when we needed his voice.

I remembered the exit when we needed grit.

I remembered that he cashed out and disappeared when it counted.

And now he wanted to stand next to the work I had bled for, as if he had built any of it.

I looked him in the eye, and said, thanks but no. I realized: the test wasn't whether he had changed. It was whether I had.

Then the messages started coming. Emails. DMs. Calls. The same voices that once withheld credit or twisted stories now wanted to reconnect. To "catch up." There was no anger in me. Just a sharper clarity. You can forgive someone and still keep the door closed. Growth doesn't mean repeating old cycles. And leadership isn't defined by how many people follow you, it's defined by who you no longer chase.

I remember one especially quiet night, walking the floor of our office after hours. Everyone had gone home. The lights were low. I sat at a small desk in the back of the screening room, surrounded by monitors, models, and half-drunk coffee cups. And it hit me: this wasn't just about surviving anymore. This was about scaling something sacred. And it needed structure.

Every surface told a story. Coffee cups. Sketches. Slack threads still open. These weren't just employees. They were lives, dreams, rent payments, late-night breakthroughs. And I was the one who set the course they were following.

So, I got obsessed. EOS. Dashboards. Process maps. Decision trees. Communication architecture. Safety protocols. Emotional health check-ins. Weekly alignment sessions that covered not just deliverables, but culture. Not just performance, but purpose.

Because at scale, misalignment compounds. But so does clarity. And clarity is what lets you move without chaos.

We had to release people. Some had been there from the beginning. That part stung. I remember sitting across from one of our earliest hires, someone I'd celebrated wins and weathered storms with. But the role had outgrown them, and they knew it. We both did. We hugged before they left. No resentment, no drama, just a quiet recognition that this chapter was over. Letting go wasn't cold. It was clear.

Growth doesn't always mean bigger.

Sometimes it means braver.

Every offboarding became a ritual in risk mitigation. We didn't just part ways. We studied what went wrong. We adjusted roles, redefined org charts, and audited responsibilities. Because I no longer saw leadership as just momentum. I saw it as architecture. If something fell apart, I didn't blame the storm, I reinforced the blueprint.

As my companies began to scale and intersect with entire industries, it became clear: this wasn't about me anymore. It wasn't even about us. It was about the systems we were setting in motion. The plaza wasn't just a dream; it was an engine. Risk mitigation wasn't a product; it was a way to empower bold moves without fear. Managing companies wasn't a duty; it was a design principle. A model for how capital, clarity, and mission can work together. These weren't vehicles for my ambition. They were vaults for shared momentum. Built not to revolve around me, but to evolve without me.

PAUSE HERE.
You've already paid the price.
You've already earned the clarity.
This next stretch isn't about becoming.
It's about integrating.
Leading not to prove, but to preserve.
Not to defend, but to define.
You're not chasing a seat at the table anymore,
you're building the room.

I stopped making decisions based only on instinct and started operating from evidence. From what we'd already proven. From what was already working. I asked better questions. "Where are we exposed?" "Where is our weakest point?" "What would break if we doubled in size tomorrow?" "If I disappeared tomorrow, would this still run?" Because real leadership isn't about being essential, it's about being unnecessary. It's about designing in a way where the vision outlives your presence.

The road back is subtle. No lights. No speeches. Just you and the next decision. And the one after that. It comes with decisions. With boundary-setting. With reintegration into a world that never expected you to return like this.

But you don't come back the same. You come back as the architect.

With scars turned into systems.

With failure turned into frameworks.

With doubt turned into discipline.

With structure designed to carry others, not just yourself.

The world will still test you. But you've already passed the hardest test: becoming the kind of leader who no longer needs to be understood.

Because now?

You don't adjust to the world.

You shape it.

.::. - The return is not a reunion.
It's a reckoning.
You've walked through the fire.
You've faced the silence.
You've released what couldn't carry.
Now you're back, not to be celebrated,
but to calibrate.
To lead from evidence.
To architect what lasts.
No spotlight. No applause.
Just structure.
Just design.
Just you…
and the system that now holds everything in place.

The
Pivot Point

*When hustle becomes architecture,
and structure starts to carry the weight.*

Chapter 10
The Shift Back

*"You don't scale by force.
You scale by alignment."*

It didn't happen in the boardroom. No tickertape. No roaring applause. Just a quiet Friday afternoon, golden light stretching across the floor like it knew something was shifting.

We were in a meeting, reviewing the details of a new vertical.

Six months earlier, a discussion like that would've set off alarms; new risks, unknown variables, fires waiting to ignite. But that day, I didn't interrupt. I just listened.

And that's when I saw it.

The team wasn't looking to me. They were solving it. Together. Not perfectly. But with rhythm. No panic. No sideways glances. No need for my permission. Just alignment.

The Shift Back

That was the moment.

It wasn't flashy. It didn't trend. But it shifted everything. I wasn't the engine anymore. I was the architect. The scaffolding had done its job, and the structure was standing on its own.

That's when I realized we had crossed the pivot point.

It didn't feel like power. It felt like a release. The shift from founder energy; adrenaline, hustle, and constant vigilance, to something deeper. Something scalable. The mission wasn't something I had to carry anymore. It could carry itself.

And the reason? We had finally stopped forcing it.

In the early days, growth looked like chaos disguised as progress. We were sprinting on fumes, saying yes to everything, new deals, new platforms, new partnerships. I remember one morning opening our dashboard and seeing it: forty-nine active projects. On paper, it looked impressive. In reality, it was a skyscraper built from duct tape and caffeine.

That morning, I shut the laptop and called an emergency leadership session.

"What is sacred?" I asked.

Silence.

Then I followed with, "What is scalable?"

That's when honesty surfaced. We'd been performing scale instead of building it. So, we cut. We delayed launches. Ended partnerships. Shut down pet projects that served the ego but not the mission.

We didn't scale by stacking more. We scaled by subtracting what didn't belong.

But the hardest pivot wasn't operational. It was personal.

I had confused leadership with presence. If a pitch deck went out without my edits, I panicked. If a decision got made without my voice, I felt threatened. I wasn't leading, I was hovering.

One day, my head of operations pulled me aside. No emotion.

Just the truth.

"You're making us wait for you. And we're losing our rhythm."

It landed like a punch. But it was also a gift.

So, I started stepping back. Slowly. From design reviews. From status calls. From approvals. At first, it felt like it was disappearing. Like I was letting go of the very thing I'd bled to build.

But then the opposite happened.

The room sharpened. Decisions got faster. People took ownership. Accountability deepened. And I watched something extraordinary unfold: they weren't just executing the plan. They were expanding it.

That's when I learned leadership isn't the loudest voice. It's the clearest alignment.

But alignment breaks if culture is chaos.

In the early days, our culture lived in late-night Slack threads and shared playlists. We felt like family. But culture that isn't defined eventually dissolves. So, we named it. We mapped our values to actions. We built onboarding around it.

When conflict hit, we didn't point fingers. We pointed to the framework.

"Where did we drift?"

We turned down top talent who didn't align. One celebrity reached out, offering to attach their name to a project for a piece of equity. The reach would've been global. But when we asked what part of our mission resonated with them, they gave us a rehearsed line about brand synergy.

We passed.

The Shift Back

Because hype can't hold weight. Systems can.

And as we grew, the company became a mirror. Every flaw I hadn't resolved in myself started showing up somewhere else. So, I stopped hiring generalists and started hiring giants, specialists who could outpace me in their zones. Operators. Architects. Legal minds. Engineers of scale.

We rolled out EOS. Built dashboards. Held quarterly reviews. Ran weekly alignment sessions, not just for tasks, but for trust. Because when you scale, misalignment multiplies. But so does clarity.

Pause here.
This is where your value shifts, not in how much you carry, but in how well others rise without you.
You've led by doing. Now it's time to lead by design.
What have you built that works... without you?

I remember one night, walking to the office after hours.

Everyone had gone home. It was quiet. The kind of quiet that lets you hear the weight of what you've built. I walked past whiteboards full of strategy, coffee cups left behind after long sprints, notes scribbled on windows. And I asked myself the question that scared me most:

"If I disappeared tomorrow, would this still run?"

Because real leadership isn't about being essential. It's about being unnecessary.

That was the final shift.

Not tactical. Emotional.

I had built my reputation on being the guy who did it all. The late-night closer. The fixer. The guy who never dropped the ball. But that version of me couldn't carry this next phase.

I had to let go of proving. Let go of performing. Let go of being "the guy."

I had to become someone who didn't just do the work but designed the environment for others to do theirs. Who made fewer moves, but bigger ones. With clarity. With precision. With purpose.

It felt like a loss.

But it was a legacy.

That's the pivot.

When the story stops being about your hustle and starts becoming about the structure that will outlast you.

When you stop building to be seen and start building to stay.

When you realize you don't scale by force, but by clarity, culture, and trust.

I'm not the engine anymore. I'm not supposed to be.

Now I'm the architect of alignment.

The steward of what remains.

And once you make that shift...

There's no going back.

This is the pivot point, when you stop needing to be essential, and start designing what could exist without you.

The Shift Back

.::. - One day, you look around and realize the machine is moving, without your push. The plan is being shaped, without your pen. And the decisions are being made, without your cue.

Not because you've vanished.

But because you've built something stronger than your presence.

You've built alignment.

And that?

That's the beginning of permanence.

The
Depth Shift

*When scaling stops being about reach,
and starts becoming about roots.*

CHAPTER 11
THE SHIFT FROM MOMENTUM TO MEANING

"You don't build empires by reaching further.
You build them by going deeper."

The beginning is always loud.
There's a rhythm to early growth: urgent, breathless, addictive.
You chase opportunities, fight fires, land wins. Every milestone feels like proof. Every pitch gets applause. The game is speed, and the prize is attention. You start believing that forward is the only direction. More markets. More launches. More reach. It feels like expansion, but it's something else: acceleration.
And then one night, the room goes quiet.
I remember sitting alone at the office, long past midnight. The walls were still. The city outside had finally stopped talking. I was tired, but not from lack of sleep. It was something deeper, a kind of ache I couldn't name. So, I

The Shift From Momentum To Meaning

laid out a map across the table. Not of cities. Not of logistics. A different kind of map. A map of responsibility.

I traced the lines with my finger: territories, industries, relationships. This wasn't about where we could go next. It was about whether we even should. It wasn't geography. It was gravity. I looked at each point not as a goal, but as a question. Did we belong here? Did we deserve to stay? Were we building something that could be trusted to last?

In those quiet hours, I realized: we weren't scaling. We were stacking. Project after project, logo after logo, deck after deck.

From the outside, it looked like momentum. On the inside, it was erosion. Our internal tracker had forty-nine active initiatives. Every single one looked sharp in a pitch, but together they pulled us off course, away from purpose, away from the soul of what we were building.

So I closed the laptop and called the leadership team. No slides. No plan. Just a question: "What is sacred?" That silence, the kind where you realize no one wants to say what they already know, that's when the work began. We started naming the things that mattered. Then we started cutting everything else. We shut down the distractions. Delayed the launches that weren't ready. Declined partnerships that didn't pass the soul check.

That wasn't just operational. That was existential. Because the next step wasn't to do more. It was to do what mattered, longer.

And that meant letting go.

Until then, I had been at the center. Every deck, every deal, every decision. It made me feel important. It made me feel in control. But in truth, it was a ceiling. We couldn't grow unless I got out of the way. So I did something harder than scaling, I disappeared. Quietly, intentionally, I began to remove myself from the center.

Entire projects were handed off. Final decisions were made without me. I wasn't on the calls. I didn't weigh in.

And for the first time, things didn't fall apart. They got stronger.

Pause here.
Not everything that looks like growth is real.
Sometimes what we call progress is just motion, momentum built on adrenaline, not alignment.
You can stack projects, expand teams, open offices...
and still be building on erosion.
More isn't always stronger. Faster isn't always better. So ask yourself:
- What are you building that's designed to last?
- What part of your momentum is actually distraction?
- Where do you need to subtract in order to deepen?
This isn't just about what's next.
It's about what's worth continuing.

One deal, I'll never forget it, closed overseas while I was across the world, completely uninvolved. It went flawlessly. The division was led by someone who had once nearly quit from burnout. But we had slowed down, invested in them, brought them into strategy. Now they ran that vertical better than I ever could have. Because we had built something real. A system, not a shrine.

The irony is that real leadership requires absence. You don't scale by holding on. You scale by letting go.

Of course, not everything worked. One expansion nearly collapsed because we misread the culture. What we thought was innovation felt like intrusion to the people on the ground. We hit pause. We listened. We brought in local advisors. We restarted, this time, with humility. That mistake taught me something I now ask every founder I mentor: What does your mission sound like in someone else's language?

If you can't answer that, you're not ready to grow.

Expansion isn't conquest. It's covenant. It's not about showing up to extract value. It's about showing up to build trust. That means understanding the soil before you plant the flag. That means asking questions before offering answers. That means showing up with curiosity, not certainty.

Every territory we entered demanded a new posture. In Los Angeles, it was about media presence. In New York, financial fluency. In Utah, sustainable impact. The South asked for history and heart.

And in each case, we didn't show up with a pitch.

We showed up with a question:

"What matters here?"

That became our culture. We brought playbooks, yes. But we also brought listening. We stopped chasing alignment on paper and started building alignment in person. New hires weren't asked, "What can you do for us?" They were asked, "What do you care about that we can build together?" And the answers reshaped everything.

One by one, we walked away from offers that didn't honor the work. Licensing deals that wanted our logo, but not our legacy. Partnerships that looked profitable but felt hollow. Global expansion deals that promised reach and would've sold out the soul of what we'd built.

We said no. Repeatedly. Not out of pride, but out of principle.

Because every "yes" adds weight. And weight, when it's not aligned, will break you. If you scale in the wrong direction, you don't grow, you fracture.

Eventually, we stopped expanding for reach and started expanding for root. New offices weren't flags. They were foundations. New partnerships weren't transactions. They were trust agreements. We weren't launching anymore. We were layering. Designing. Embedding. Not to dominate, but to endure.

That's when it hit me: the adrenaline was gone. And I didn't miss it.

What replaced it was deeper. Stronger. Quieter. We weren't performing. We were planting. And what we planted, in systems, in people, in culture, started growing on its own. I remember watching a screen one afternoon, reviewing dailies. The team was in full swing. Everyone in rhythm. I wasn't even needed that day. And for the first time in my life, that wasn't threatening. That was peace.

Because that's the shift no one talks about, when you stop proving and start preserving. When your job stops being to run ahead and starts being to hold the core. When you realize that empire isn't about reach. It's about depth. Not how many people know your name. But how many carry your values when you're not in the room.

The empire doesn't need more territory.

It needs more trust.

And trust takes time.

It takes listening.

It takes letting go.

So if you're building, really building, ask yourself:

Where are you pretending to scale when you're actually just sprinting?

What are you stacking instead of strengthening?

Can your mission survive without your name attached to it?

Because someday, if you've done it right, your greatest contribution won't be what you control. It will be what continues without you.

And that's not the end.

That's the reward.

The Shift From Momentum To Meaning

.::. - You used to run the room.

Not because you craved attention, but because everything depended on you. Your energy. Your insight. Your willpower. You were the engine. The firefighter. The force that kept the mission alive.

But something changed.

Now you walk into the office and the rhythm is already in motion. Questions get answered. Problems get solved. And no one looks to you for approval, because they don't need to. You built it that way.

This is the shift.

Not away from leadership, but into a deeper version of it.

Not louder. Wiser.

The adrenaline is gone, and you don't miss it.

Because now your greatest contribution isn't what you do. It's what happens when you're not in the room. The systems you designed. The standards you upheld. The people who learned to move with clarity because you gave them the blueprint, not just the orders.

You're not sprinting anymore.

You're anchoring.

And the reward?

It's not in reach.

It's in roots.

You stopped building to be everywhere.

And started building what can outlast you, anywhere.

The
Center Hold

*When speed fades and systems are strained,
this is where structure proves its worth.*

Chapter 12
The Hardest Part No One Talks About

*"Leadership isn't just what you build,
it's what you hold together
when everything pulls apart."*

The public celebrates expansion. New cities, big hires, product launches. All signals of progress. But what comes after the applause? That's where the real work begins.

There's a phase nobody talks about. Not the launch. Not the scale. The part after. The part where everything is technically working, and yet somehow, things feel like they're unraveling. Not in a dramatic crash, but in a quiet drift.

Consolidation.

It doesn't trend. It doesn't photograph well. But it is the most essential chapter of growth. The moment when speed gives way to weight. When leadership shifts from momentum to maintenance. From charisma to clarity.

The Hardest Part No One Talks About

From spark to engine. And when the business either stabilizes... or splinters.

We looked great on paper. Expanding footprint, multiple regions, rising revenue. But under the surface? Friction. Teams operating in silos. Systems strained past their original design. What worked when we were twenty people was breaking at two hundred. What was once fast and fluid now took three meetings and five approvals.

One moment snapped the illusion. We were onboarding a new partner. Everyone showed up prepared, deck, docs, schedule. But halfway through the call, I realized two of our senior team members, key ones, had never even met. They were executing the same initiative across different continents, using different playbooks. They weren't misaligned. They were disconnected.

That wasn't a talent problem. It was a systems problem. It was a leadership problem. It was my problem.

Consolidation required a new kind of focus. Not on what we were building, but how it was held together. How decisions traveled. How culture translated. How the values echoed through distance and scale. The question wasn't "Can we grow more?" It became "Can we grow without splintering?"

What followed was harder than any launch I'd ever done.

We had people, good people, who had been vital in the early days. Warriors. Builders. Problem solvers. But the complexity of consolidation had left them exposed. Their roles didn't fit anymore. Some slowed down decisions. Others created confusion. Their instincts were gold in chaos but misaligned in scale.

There was one conversation that still sticks with me. A teammate I deeply respected, who had carried us through more storms than I could count. But lately? Their seat had become a bottleneck. I knew it. They knew it. We sat on a

Zoom call in silence, both dreading the words we had to say. I offered a new seat. They declined. We hugged through the screen. It was respectful. It was right. And it broke my heart.

That's the part of leadership no one writes about.

Loyalty without alignment is not kindness. It's cruelty, slowly choking the mission, the team, even the person you're trying to protect. Sometimes, the kindest thing you can do is set someone free from the version of the company they helped build.

And so, we restructured. We reassigned. We released. Not out of punishment. Out of preservation. We weren't just a business anymore; we were a system. And systems don't run on sentiment. They run on structure.

I had to evolve again. Not as the builder. Not even as the leader. But as the architect. Because scale isn't just size. It's structure that doesn't crumble when you let go.

That meant operational playbooks. Escalation ladders. Conflict protocols. Chain of command. Culture audits. Communication cadence. Trust that wasn't assumed, it was engineered.

It wasn't sexy. But it was sustainable.

And in the quiet of that shift, I felt something else. The loneliness.

The adrenaline of early wins had faded. I wasn't needed in the same way. I found myself proud, and restless. I'd sit in strategy meetings where things were handled without me. Deals closed without my touch. The machine was running. And still, I wrestled with the urge to step back in, just to feel important.

But I knew the cost. If I jumped in just to feel needed, I'd break the very systems we built to survive without me. I had to let go.

There was a brutal week when everything stalled. Three critical deals in limbo. An operations restructure frozen.

Even our marketing pipeline stood still. And every delay? It traced back to me.

I wasn't micromanaging. But I hadn't transitioned. I was the bottleneck.

That's when I made the shift. I engineered myself out of the center. Weekly strategy cadence. Vision only. No more approvals. No more touchpoints unless invited. My new job wasn't to drive, it was to observe, refine, and protect the signal.

Pause here.
If you disappeared for 30 days,
would your business survive or stall?
Would your absence expose gaps… or reveal strength?
This is where leadership stops being presence,
and becomes architecture.

Let go. Watch what holds. That's the real test.
And if it cracks? Good. Now you know where to reinforce.

And when I stepped back?

Speed returned. Ownership deepened. The rhythm clicked.

One day we had a total outage in one of our regions. Systems down. Client delays. Old me would've dropped everything. This time? I watched as the team activated protocols, rerouted workflows, kept the brand intact.

That's when I knew: the center held.

Because that's the test of consolidation. Not just if the business survives a storm, but whether it gets stronger because of it.

So, ask yourself:
- Where are you still the bottleneck, not because they need you, but because you haven't let go?
- What role are you holding onto because it validates you, even if it slows the mission?

- Have you designed a business that depends on your energy, or one that thrives without it?

This isn't the phase where you make headlines. It's where you prove you deserve the ones you already earned.

You don't consolidate to slow down. You consolidate to make sure the next level doesn't kill the culture.

You consolidate to make the center unshakable.

And when the storm comes, and it always comes, it's not the brand, the product, or the hype that determines whether you survive.

It's what you've built at the core.

If the center holds, everything else can be rebuilt.

If the center holds, you don't have to be the center anymore.

You've already done your job.

Now let the structure do its work.

The Hardest Part No One Talks About

.::. - You built it. You led it. You carried it through fire.
But the hardest part? Letting go without letting it fall.
This is where you become something more:
Not the heartbeat, but the spine.
You step back, not because you're less needed,
but because what you built is finally strong enough to stand.
This is consolidation. Quiet. Uncelebrated.
But it's what makes scale real.
Ask less, "Am I still essential?"
Ask more, "Will this still endure?"

The
Uplift

*When the climb ends,
the carry begins.*

Chapter 13
The Shift From Growth To Uplift

*"You don't rise by climbing higher.
You rise by lifting more with you."*

You think the story ends when you scale. When the business stabilizes, the team runs without you, and the systems click into place. But that's not the finish line. That's the threshold.

The real ascent doesn't begin with more; it begins with meaning.

One evening, long after the expansion had solidified and the storm of consolidation had passed, I sat alone in the quiet of our main office. Lights low. No fires to put out. No calls waiting. Just me, a cup of cold coffee, and a whiteboard still half-filled from a strategy meeting earlier that day.

And a question came. One I hadn't asked in a while.

Now that we've built this... what's it for?

We had the numbers. The market reach. The credibility. But was that it? Was that the peak?

I thought about the people we'd mentored, the partnerships we'd formed, the founders we'd advised quietly on weekends. I remembered one in particular, a first-time entrepreneur who, after our session, looked me dead in the eye and said, "I didn't know someone like me could build something like this."

That sentence shook something in me.

Pause here:
You've built something that works.
But now the question is:
Does it lift anyone but you?
The goal was never just growth.
It was gravity.
Are people rising because of your presence...
or your structure?
And when you step back,
do others step up?

This phase wasn't about height anymore. It was about gravity. About pull. About turning altitude into access.

Elevation, I realized, isn't about how far you can climb. It's about how many others you can lift while you're up there.

So, we changed how we told the story. I stopped being the protagonist. The team was. The mission was. The community was. I began sharing the stage; loudly, deliberately. Credit became currency. Visibility became empowerment.

And something remarkable happened: people rose. Not because I told them to. But because I got out of the way.

There's a myth in business that legacy comes from the name on the building. That permanence means preserving yourself in stone. But the longer I led, the clearer it became: legacy is the systems you leave behind. Not statues. Systems. Missions that run when you're gone. Values that hold when no one's watching.

We started investing differently. Built succession pipelines. Funded education programs. Backed creative labs and small-business accelerators. We formed partnerships not to acquire, but to amplify. We built initiatives not for ROI, but for ROE - Return on Empowerment.

That's when we stopped building a business and started building institutions.

I let go of more equity. Gave seats at the table to unexpected voices. Created governance structures with customers, not just executives. We opened the platform. And the platform opened new possibilities.

I didn't need to own everything. I needed to align everyone.

And when you do that, when you create a system where people feel entrusted instead of managed, the work deepens. People start showing up not because they're paid, but because they believe.

This wasn't about going public. It was about going permanent.

There were moments that sealed this shift for me, quiet ones, never the headline kind.

A deal signed in another country by a team I hadn't talked to in months, because they no longer needed permission. A community partnership I only learned about after it launched, because people were thinking like owners. A mentee I once advised becoming an advisor to someone else, because impact had created inheritance.

And I thought, This is it.

This is what it means to elevate: to disappear from the center but multiply your influence at the edges.

But even elevation has weight.

At that height, the air gets thinner. Fewer people understand the choices. Misinterpretation increases. The margin for error narrows. Every word, every action, becomes precedent. The higher you go, the further your shadow can reach.

So, we slowed down again. Simplified decision chains. Flattened anything that could be flat. Offloaded ego. Built tools that made the mission lighter to carry.

And I had to lead lighter, too. Less speaking. More listening. Less steering. More designing.

I started asking better questions: Who does this serve? What precedent does this set? If this became standard, would we be proud?

We didn't build a tower. We built a skybridge.

Because at that level, you're not just building for scale. You're building for signal. Everything you do becomes a message to the future.

You start thinking in echoes.

I used to think the goal was to get to the top. Now I know the top doesn't exist. What exists is the view. The vantage point to pull others up. To stretch a hand forward and another backward.

And now the real question is yours to answer:
- Who are you lifting?
- What systems are you leaving?
- Are you still the center, or have you become the signal?

Because the measure of a leader isn't how high you climb.

It's how many rise with you.

.::. - You've scaled. You've stabilized. You've stepped back.
Now comes the work no one claps for: lifting others higher than you stood.
It's not about being seen anymore.
It's about being the reason someone else believes they can be.
Legacy isn't presence.
It's permission.
Not what you kept, but what you gave.
Not the title, but the trust.
And the question that lingers now...
Who rises because you already did?

The
Sacred Handoff

*When leadership becomes legacy,
and presence gives way to permanence.*

Chapter 14
How To Leave Without Losing Yourself

*"The end is never the end.
It's just when the story changes hands."*

Most people chase the exit like a finish line. They call it the goal, the dream, the moment you cash in and coast. But I've learned something different.

The exit isn't the end.

It's the test.

You spend years building something from breath. You carry it on your shoulders when no one else can see it. You sacrifice, stretch, burn, and rebuild, over and over, until the thing has weight of its own. Until the dream becomes a machine. And then, just when it finally runs without friction, the world asks you the hardest question: Can you let it go?

Not because it's failing. But because it's thriving.

How To Leave Without Losing Yourself

For me, the signs came softly. Not in a crisis or confrontation. Just a slow shift. Meetings that didn't need me. Decisions that didn't include me. Celebrations where I was no longer the one being toasted. The center began to stretch, and I wasn't in it.

At first, I told myself it was by design. And it was. I had built systems to run without me. Leaders who didn't need translation.

Culture that could stand on its own. That was the point.

But knowing that and feeling it are two different things.

There was a night, quiet, past midnight. I was the only one left in the office. The screens were dark. The hallway lights buzzed. I sat with my hands folded, no notes to write, no fires to put out, no one waiting for an answer.

And the silence asked me: Who are you now?

I had built this thing to outlive me. I preached redundancy, sustainability, systems over personality. But somewhere along the way, I had still tied my worth to being in the middle of it.

That night, I started the real work. Not of leaving the company, but of exiting the identity I had built inside it. I didn't want to vanish. I wanted to evolve.

But evolution isn't automatic. It takes intention. It takes structure. And most of all, it takes time.

Pause here.
You can't exit what still defines you.
Letting go isn't about leaving. It's about what you leave behind.
So ask yourself:
Have you built something that can breathe without you?
Or are you still the oxygen?

We began mapping it out, an 18-month transition. Not just in title, but in truth. I mentored the leaders who would lead without me. I handed off decisions, then authority, then ownership of the outcomes. We wrote handbooks, trained successors, turned culture into codified rituals.

And slowly, the room changed.

They stopped asking, What would he say? and started declaring, Here's how we do it.

That's how you know you've built something real.

But there were days I grieved.

You don't just step out of the center without feeling the absence. I'd wake up and check the calendars I wasn't on. Open documents I wasn't needed in. Watch from the sidelines as rooms I used to command moved on without my voice.

There were moments of weightlessness. Like I had pressed "send" on a part of my identity and now stood waiting for the bounce-back.

But grief eventually gave way to something else. Not relief. Not release.

Pride.

I remember watching one of our newest directors lead a global strategy call. Clear. Confident. Aligned. They handled it with more grace and clarity than I had at that stage. And I realized something:

I wasn't watching the company forget me.

I was watching the company fulfill me.

Legacy doesn't live in the spotlight. It lives in the shadows, the systems, the choices, the invisible fingerprints on a culture that moves without instruction.

You don't control how you're remembered. You don't control what happens after the handoff. But you do control the depth of what you embed.

I stopped focusing on the headline and started focusing on the margins. Not what would be seen, but what would be felt. The principles tucked into onboarding. The values hidden in how we disagree. The decisions that echo through people I'll never meet.

That's real succession. Not a replacement. A relay.

And what no one tells you is that a good exit isn't a disappearance.

It's a gift.

You create space. Space for others to rise. Space for the culture to mature. Space for the mission to grow louder than your voice.

And in that space, something else happens.

You begin again.

Not because you're unfinished. But because builders don't stop. We just move to new foundations. New blueprints. New canvases. Not smaller, deeper.

So, if you're staring down your own version of an exit, ask yourself:

Are you holding on out of fear? Or are you staying out of service?

Have you built something that needs you?

Or something that frees you?

The exit isn't the end. It's the most sacred handoff you'll ever make.

And if you do it right… the story continues, stronger than before.

Without you in the middle.

But because of you at the start.

.::. - You won't always be the one holding the mic.
Or the marker. Or the map.
And that's the point.
Because the greatest measure of your leadership isn't what you held onto.
It's what you embedded deep enough to be carried by others.
Not every exit needs a spotlight.
Some need silence.
The kind that leaves room for new voices to rise.
When done right, the handoff isn't an ending.
It's a new beginning, powered by a foundation only you could lay.
So the question isn't: What are they building without you?
It's: Did you build well enough for them to build better?

The
Living Legacy

*When impact is passed forward,
not left behind.*

Chapter 15
Legacy In Real Time

"Legacy isn't what you leave behind. It's what you pass forward while you're still here."

By the time I reached the other side of the exit, something had shifted. The urgency was gone. The noise, quieter. The calendar felt lighter. The calls less constant. But one question kept circling, silent at first, then louder each week: What now?

Not what's next. But what matters right now.

That question doesn't get answered in pitch decks or board retreats. It gets answered in the quiet. In slow mornings. In long walks without a destination. It shows up in the spaces where ambition used to live. Where you stop trying to prove and start trying to pour. Where success is no longer a finish line, but a responsibility.

Legacy In Real Time

Legacy isn't a headline. It's not a farewell speech. It's not the number of people who show up when you leave. It's the number who grew while you stayed.

One of those realizations came unexpectedly. I was invited to a summit. I declined the keynote but said I'd attend. Quietly. I sat in the back of the room. No badge. No spotlight. A former intern, now a CEO, stood on stage. She told her story. And buried in her talk was a moment I had long forgotten. A conversation. A sentence. Something I said offhand that had taken root in her life. "If no one opens the door, build your own. Just don't forget to hold it open for the next one coming up behind you."

That's what I'd said.

I barely remembered saying it.

But she remembered everything.

She built something.

She hired people.

She mentored a team.

She held the door open.

She didn't know I was in the room. And I didn't need her to.

That's when I felt it: not pride, but peace.

In that moment I understood:

You don't always get to witness your impact. But if you lead right, it shows up anyway, in someone else's story.

Ask yourself:

- What if the thing that changes someone's life isn't a master plan or a grand gesture, but one sentence you forgot you even said?
- What if your real legacy isn't what you build, but what you awaken in someone else?

There was a season when my name was on everything.

Headlines.

Proposals.

Strategy decks.

And then came the season when it wasn't. My role shifted from visible to vital. From leading to lifting. People didn't call for approval anymore. They called for perspective. Not for money, but for clarity. And I realized, this is legacy. Not being remembered but being useful.

Legacy isn't made of wins. It's made of weight. Of what you're willing to carry forward when no one's clapping. I started checking in with people I hadn't spoken to in years. Not because I needed something. But because I remembered what it felt like to be in their seat. I made a list of mentors I hadn't thanked properly and started calling them one by one. And I showed up for first-time founders who reminded me of myself: tired, stretched, unsure.

I didn't need to be the one on stage. I needed to be the one holding the light.

Pause here.
The impact isn't always loud.
Legacy doesn't need credit.
But it does need presence.
Right now, someone is watching how you carry the weight.
Ask yourself:
What will they remember:
the noise of your wins,
or the steadiness of your presence?

At some point, the torch isn't handed off. It's set down gently for someone else to pick up. I started teaching. Not in seminars. In car rides. Dinners. Whiteboard sessions that turned into therapy. I didn't tell them the wins. I told them the truth.

The launches that flopped.
The friends who ghosted.
The deals that drained my soul.

Legacy In Real Time

The decisions that cost me sleep.

Because if you only pass forward your highlight reel, you're not preparing the next generation, you're misleading them.

So I started documenting what no one told me. How to say no when the money is right, but the mission is wrong. How to protect your mental health without apologizing. How to lead a team when you feel like you're the one falling apart. These were the facts that had kept me upright. They became the toolkit I handed down.

Because in the end, everything we build becomes someone else's to carry. And if we've done it right, they'll carry more than just the structure, they'll carry the spirit. And the only real question is: Will it last?

That became my obsession. I went back to every entity I'd ever touched and asked one brutal question: If I vanished tomorrow, would this still stand? If not, why? What needed shoring up? What wasn't documented? Who was still relying on memory over method?

We rewrote charters. Rebuilt systems. Embedded values into everyday decisions; not slogans, but habits. Legacy isn't carved in stone. It's built into culture.

And the deeper your legacy, the lighter your ego. You stop needing credit. You start needing continuity. You stop asking who noticed. You start asking who grew.

There was a night, late, when a young founder called me. She was in tears. "I think I'm failing," she said. I told her the truth: "No. You're carrying something heavy for the first time. And that's not failure. That's leadership."

That's what they need us for. Not advice. Presence.

Living legacy is not about what you build. It's about how you show up when the cameras are off. It's presence in silence.

Kindness in pressure. Faith when it's easier to quit. It's doing the invisible work that gives others permission to be visible.

So I keep showing up. Not to build another empire. Not to make another headline. But to imprint something that lives deeper than recognition.

Because if you build the right way, what you leave behind won't just carry your name.

It will carry your integrity.

Your clarity.

Your courage.

Your character.

And your questions.

So, ask yourself:

- What would still stand if your name were no longer attached?
- Who are you mentoring that has nothing to offer you in return?
- What truths are you keeping quiet that someone else needs to hear out loud?
- Where are you still clinging to be seen, when you're supposed to be supporting?
- Have you built something that serves your ego, or your absence?

Legacy isn't a monument. It's a message.

And if you've built it right, it will outlive the memory of your face, but not the memory of your impact.

So build quietly.

Teach fully.

Let go slowly.

And live it now.

Because legacy isn't waiting for the end.

It's whispering in every decision you make today.

.::. - You might not recognize the moment when legacy begins.

It doesn't arrive with a speech or a spotlight. It slips in quietly, on an ordinary day, in the middle of a meeting you didn't call, during a conversation you're not leading.

Someone quotes something you forgot you said.

Someone makes a decision rooted in a value you once modeled.

And you realize they're growing, without your help, without your permission. Not because you told them what to do, but because you showed them how.

That's legacy.

Not a monument, but a movement that continues without your name attached.

It's the systems that hold when you're gone. The courage that spreads through people you never met.

It's not about the company you built, it's about the people who build because of you. Quietly. Boldly.

Because you made it safe to try.

Because you showed up before it was easy.

So take a moment.

Look around.

Ask yourself:

Who's watching how you carry the weight?

Who's learning from how you listen, how you lead, how you let go?

Because the most enduring thing you'll ever leave behind isn't a building or a brand, it's belief.

Belief that they can lead too.

And that's the real legacy: not what you leave when you're done, but what they carry forward while you're still here.

The
Trail Behind You

*What you blaze forward...
becomes the path for others.*

Chapter 16
The Weight Of The Torch

*"The gift isn't what you take with you.
It's what you come back to give."*

The journey changed me. That much is undeniable. But transformation was never the destination, it was the toll. The price I had to pay to bring something back. Because if the climb only serves the climber, it's not elevation. It's isolation.

I used to think the reward was the view. The summit. The breathless moment where you stand above it all. But that's not the reward. That's the proof. The reward is the responsibility. To turn around. To reach back. To walk someone else up the mountain you nearly didn't survive.

The return didn't come with fanfare. No spotlights. No second exit. It started quietly. A late-night call from a founder on the edge of burnout. A text from a young business owner whose partner had just blindsided her. A boardroom invite, not for capital, but for clarity. They didn't want my status. They wanted my stillness.

That's when I knew I had returned.

People weren't looking to me for what I had built. They were looking to me for what I had become.

So, I showed up. Not with scripts or checklists. With stories. Scars. Questions. Frameworks that had been earned the hard way. And most of all, permission. Permission to try. To break. To rebuild. To move at their own pace. I didn't give advice. I gave space.

Because the highest version of mentorship isn't giving answers.

It's restoring dignity.

That's the quiet power of the return: you stop being the main character in your own story, and you start becoming the catalyst in someone else's.

And the circle expands.

Legacy isn't linear. It's circular. What you pour into others finds its way back, not to elevate you, but to elevate all of us. I started watching people I once mentored become mentors themselves.

Not duplicates of me, but upgrades. Leading lighter. Building better. Asking braver questions.

The final stage of the journey isn't mastery. It's multiplication.

I still remember when one of them sent me a photo. Launch day. A small team, standing in front of their first office, grinning like they had just climbed Everest, and maybe they had. I didn't feel pride. I felt peace. Because in that moment, I wasn't looking at my legacy.

I was looking at theirs.

The greatest gift I could offer wasn't capital. It wasn't strategy. It was belief. In their voice. In their vision. In their right to do it differently. So I stopped walking in with solutions. I started walking in with better questions.

And when you ask better questions, something extraordinary happens: people rise.

I began to build new rooms. Not rooms where I stood at the front, but rooms where no one needed a stage. Rooms where curiosity was currency. Where questions held more weight than answers. Where someone could walk in unsure and walk out clear.

I remember thinking, this is what I was building all along. Not an empire, but a skybridge. A structure others could cross. A way to bring people from potential to purpose, without the toll of loneliness.

Because the right room changes everything.

And so I ask:

What are you building that still scares you?

What part of your journey are you still trying to hide that someone else desperately needs to hear?

Who are you mentoring that won't benefit you at all?

The return isn't about relevance. It's about resonance. You come back not to be seen, but to be of use. Not to reclaim the spotlight, but to set the stage. Because if your wisdom dies with you, it was never wisdom. It was vanity.

I started creating cohorts. Quiet gatherings. Fireside conversations. Places where leaders could sharpen each other, not perform for each other. Where younger versions of me; awkward, earnest, overwhelmed, wouldn't feel out of place. They'd feel called up.

Because if the best of us keep showing up in better rooms, the future doesn't just happen.

It's designed.

Legacy In Real Time

Pause here.
There's a moment after the climb
where the silence hits differently.
Not because you're lost.
But because you've arrived at something deeper.
You're no longer chasing. You're returning.
Not for the spotlight, but for the hand you once needed.
Not to take the stage, but to give it away.
So pause here.
And ask yourself:
Who are you showing up for...
that might not know how much they need you yet?

I've learned that the journey doesn't end when you let go. It deepens when you return. The reward isn't the platform. It's the invitation to build platforms for others. The opportunity to become the person you once needed. To turn your experience into a compass. Your mistakes into maps. Your scars into strategies.

Because at the end of it all, the point was never what you could take with you.

It's what you could come back and give away.

And if you've made that turn, if you've stopped climbing long enough to reach back for someone else, then you already know:

You're not at the end.
You're just getting started.
The torch was never meant to burn alone.
It was meant to light the path.
To pass warmth.
To spark more fires.
Let your wisdom become water.
Something others can drink from.
Not something kept bottled on a shelf.

Because the real weight of the torch... is not in carrying it.

It's in offering its light, again and again, to those still finding their way.

Legacy In Real Time

.::. - You won't always feel the weight of what you carry.
It won't always burn your hands or keep you up at night.
Sometimes, it's quieter than that.
It's the torch you hold, not just to see, but to share.
You'll walk into a room and find someone looking at you, not for answers,
but for proof that it's possible.
You won't need to speak first.
Your presence will speak louder.
And your wisdom, if offered gently, will be the fire that helps them rise.
You'll realize then that the reward of the journey
was never in what you built for yourself,
but in what you can now pass on, with clarity, humility, and care.
That's the real weight of the torch.
Not to hold it tightly.
But to hold it out,
so someone else can find their way home.

The
Second Start

*Because real endings
always make room for something new.*

Epilogue
The Beginning

"Endings are only beginnings wearing different clothes."

This was never just about business.

It was about becoming.

About burning away the noise until all that remained was signal. About building systems that aligned with your soul. About leading in a way that outlasts you. About realizing that the climb was never about the view, it was about who you had to become to make the return possible.

And now...

Now it's your turn!

Maybe you're just getting started. Maybe you're somewhere in the messy middle. Or maybe you've already summited, and you're wondering what comes after the applause.

The answer? Responsibility. Rhythm. Return.

The Beginning

Because success isn't the peak. It's what you do after. It's how you carry others. It's what you build when no one's watching. And it's what you pass forward while you're still here.

This book isn't a map.

It is a mirror.

It is not about my story.

It is about preparing you to write yours.

So go, build what only you can build.

Lead the way only you can lead.

And when your time comes... when you've earned your scars and carried your own weight...

Don't just remember this story.

Add to it.

Because the future doesn't belong to the loudest voice.

It belongs to the clearest signal.

To the most aligned builders.

To those who return with the gift.

The world doesn't just need more success stories.

It needs more stewards.

So own the future. Not for power. But for purpose.

Because it's not waiting for someone else.

If you're still in the fog, keep going.

If you're halfway up the mountain, dig in.

If you're nearing the summit, start building something worth leaving behind.

It's waiting for you.

Not to be claimed.

But to be carried.

Own the future.

Maybe the greatest power isn't in the steps you took, but in the space you've cleared for someone else to walk.

That's what this has been. Not a blueprint.
A becoming.
Not a final word,
but a quiet handoff.

You're still here.
Most readers stop when the story ends.
But you didn't.
That's why this next part is for you.
What follows isn't more advice, it's a compass.
A toolkit to return to when the road gets unclear, the vision gets heavy, or the climb starts to wobble.

> ➤ *An expanded version of this toolkit, with deeper questions, new frameworks, and guided exercises, is available for those who join our private Discord and email list. You can register through: http://www.klrenner.com.*

APPENDIX I
TOOLS FOR THE JOURNEY

The Creators Compass

This appendix is your reference map. It collects a few questions for reflection from each chapter to revisit, reframe, and reapply at every stage of your journey. Use them often. Let them evolve with you.

Chapter 1
- What belief are you currently holding that might be holding you back?
- What fear are you pretending isn't there?

Chapter 2
- What part of your story are you still ashamed to tell?
- How would your path change if you saw your scars as assets?

Chapter 3
- What kind of empire are you building, and who is it for?
- Where are you pretending to be smaller than you are?

Chapter 4
- What system or institution shaped your thinking, and is it still serving you?
- Where might you be unconsciously upholding something you meant to dismantle?

Chapter 5
- Who are you building with that you wouldn't re-invite if you started again tomorrow?
- What are you calling "loyalty" that might actually be fear of starting fresh?

Chapter 6
- What version of success did you inherit, and is it still yours?
- Where do you need to break your own mold?

Chapter 7
- What is your non-negotiable, and are you actually living by it?
- Where have you been tolerating misalignment?

Chapter 8
- Where do you still feel the need to prove yourself?
- What would change if you moved from proving to providing?

Chapter 9
- What mask are you still wearing to make others comfortable?
- Where do you need to reclaim your power without apology?

Chapter 10
- Where are you still building from hustle instead of alignment?
- If you disappeared tomorrow, would what you've built still run?

Chapter 11
- Where are you pretending to scale?
- Are you building something that runs with you, or without you?

Chapter 12
- What would break if you stepped back right now?
- Where are you the bottleneck without realizing it?

Chapter 13
- Who are you investing in that doesn't benefit you?
- What truths are you keeping to yourself that someone else needs to hear?

Chapter 14
- What are you holding onto that you no longer need to carry?
- What would your exit look like if it wasn't about ego?

Chapter 15
- What would still stand if your name was no longer attached?
- What lesson do you wish someone had told you earlier, and who can you tell now?

Chapter 16
- What part of your journey are you still trying to hide that someone else needs to hear?
- Who are you mentoring that won't benefit you at all?

The Journey for the Creators
1. The Call: A whisper of potential. A problem you can't ignore. A vision only you seem to see.
2. The Chaos: Everything breaks. Systems fail. Confidence wavers. The world pushes back.
3. The Climb: You start again. This time with scar tissue, not just dreams. You commit.
4. The Crisis: An identity fracture. You are forced to evolve or evaporate.
5. The Clarity: You stop chasing everything. You start choosing what matters.
6. The Construction: The real work begins. Systems. Teams. Trust. Alignment.
7. The Return: You come back changed. Not to take, but to give.
8. The Legacy: You pass it forward. Not just a name, but a way of building that lasts.

Practices:
- Quarterly offsites for reflection and re-alignment
- Weekly journaling with one key question in focus
- Monthly review of team clarity and cultural drift
- Annual 'zero-base' review of commitments and calendars

APPENDIX II
THE FAILURE PLAYBOOK

"Success teaches style.
Failure teaches structure."

This is not a warning. It's a structure.

Every failure you survive has something to teach you, if you have the discipline to document it.

Most people don't.

They move on too fast, bury the lesson under shame, or rewrite it as someone else's fault.

This playbook is how you make sure the pain wasn't wasted.

These are the tools, frameworks, and rules that came from my worst moments: bankruptcy, betrayal, collapse, commingled accounts, wrong hires, wrong partnerships, and building ladders I didn't want to climb.

Each one is a scar turned into a system.

Use this not to avoid failure, but to absorb it without being destroyed.

The Conviction Audit
"If you say 'I think,' stop."

Before every major decision:
- Do I know this, or do I just feel it?
- Can I articulate the why behind this in one sentence?
- If this fails, do I understand where the fault line will be?

Red Flag Words to eliminate:
"I guess..."
"Probably..."
"We'll figure it out..."
If you can't replace it with clarity, don't move yet.

The Failure Map
"Every collapse leaves a trail. Follow it."

When something breaks:
- Name the Outcome: What exactly failed?
- Isolate the Trigger: What was the first missed signal?
- Trace the Pattern: Where else have you seen this before?
- Extract the Lesson: What system (or standard) could have prevented it?
- Design the Guardrail: What policy, protocol, or process needs to exist now?

Repeat this after every major setback.
Make it a ritual. Not a reaction.

The 4R Filter
***"You don't build to look good.
You build to hold under pressure."***

Every plan, internal or external, must pass the 4R Filter:
- Resilience: Can it absorb impact?
- Redundancy: Are there backups for key people, systems, and tools?
- Role Clarity: Does everyone know exactly what they own?
- Real-Time Response: If something breaks, do we have a protocol?

If any answer is unclear, slow down.
Because speed without structure is sabotage.

The Emotional Stall Check
"Emotion is a signal, not a strategy."

When you're overwhelmed, under-resourced, or angry, ask:
- Am I trying to fix the problem or the feeling?
- What decision here is being made just to reduce discomfort?
- Will this still be the right move in 72 hours?

If the answer is "I'm not sure," pause.
Emotion makes great fuel.
Terrible foundation.

The Equity Filter
"Don't confuse potential with proof."

Before giving equity, title, or long-term access:
- Has this person proven capacity under pressure?
- Are they aligned with the mission, or just the momentum?
- If I had to rebuild from scratch, would I still bring them?

Every rushed partnership I regretted skipped this.
Don't hire hope. Hire history.

The Debrief Loop
"We don't 'move on.' We document."

Every quarter, run a structured failure review:
- What broke? Not what failed, but what bent before it did.
- What changed? What did we react to instead of anticipate?
- What surprised us? Surprises = blind spots.
- What did we ignore? This is often the most expensive line of the review.

Then create one new system, policy, or question to prevent it from happening again.

Do this relentlessly.

Final Rule: Build for the Collapse

You will be betrayed.
You will run out of money.
You will miss something obvious.
You will lose someone you trusted.
And when that happens, your success will be measured by one thing: Did your system hold?
You don't build to impress.
You build to protect.
That's not fear.
That's leadership.

Appendix III
The Architect's Journal

10 Prompts For The Builder Who Is Still Becoming

This isn't a workbook. It's a reckoning.
Not a challenge. A confrontation.
Use this journal when the noise gets loud. When the mission feels fragile. When the climb feels like it's building you and breaking you at the same time. These are not daily prompts.
They are decision points. Come back to them often.

The Fog Phase - When it's just belief
1. What part of your vision are you still editing to make others comfortable?
2. Who are you building with that you wouldn't re-invite if you started over tomorrow?
3. What do you know in your gut that you're pretending not to see yet?

The Climb Phase - When the pressure hits
4. Where is your leadership still built on personality instead of structure?
5. Who still has access to your time but not your trust?
6. What system is running on your energy, and how long before it breaks?
7. What compromise are you calling "strategy" that might be self-sabotage?

The Return Phase - When you're no longer the center
8. If you vanished tomorrow, what would still stand, and what would collapse?
9. What lesson are you still carrying that someone else needs to hear out loud?
10. Where have you become the ceiling, when you were meant to be the scaffolding?

These aren't just journal prompts.

They're checkpoints on the builder's journey.

Use them to audit your clarity, your culture, and your capacity to lead without burning out.

Because the future doesn't belong to the loudest voice.

It belongs to the clearest builder.

VISUAL FRAMEWORK: THE JOURNEY FOR BUILDER'S

*This diagram summarizes
the journey explored in these pages,
from calling to clarity,
from collapse to return.*

Each builder walks through this arc, again and again.
But with each cycle, the foundation grows stronger,
The reach grows wider, and the impact grows deeper.

This isn't just a book, it's a blueprint. What you've read traces a pattern found in every meaningful journey of growth, clarity, and reinvention. This framework captures that path visually, for builders who are still mid-climb, still questioning, still choosing to return with a gift. Use it not just to reflect, but to orient. Not as a destination, but as a compass.

www.ingramcontent.com/pod-product-compliance
Lightning Source LLC
Chambersburg PA
CBHW030452100526
44580CB00006B/92/J